a Wisdom

a quest for meaning in
a divided world

©hristopher

Published by Beyond Books
PO Box 48270, Kommetjie, 7976, South Africa

First edition, first impression August 2002

Edited by **Jacquie**

Design & layout by **Miche**

Cover photography by **Brian**

Printed and bound by Mills Litho, Maitland, Cape Town

ISBN 0-620-29170-2

CONTENTS

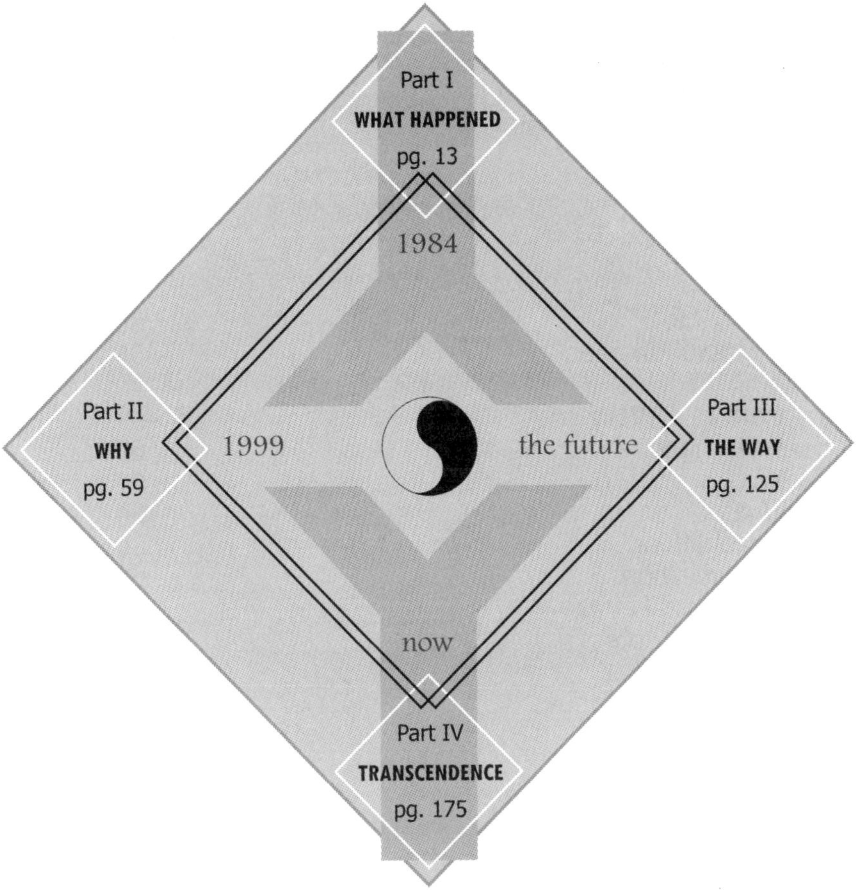
Part I
WHAT HAPPENED
pg. 13
1984
Part II
WHY
pg. 59
1999
the future
Part III
THE WAY
pg. 125
now
Part IV
TRANSCENDENCE
pg. 175

ART & ILLUSTRATIONS

For Miche . . .
who completes the circle.

ACKNOWLEDGEMENTS

As always, it is teamwork that prevails...

I'd like to thank:

Dorian for his zen-like directional guidance early on;

Sharon for her honest editorial comments;

Greg for his valued and comprehensive input;

Jill for her feedback and pointers on aspects of eastern thinking;

Ray for his inspirational enthusiasm and plot advice;

Pat for her feedback and sharing of the manuscript with her book club;

Ellen for her wisdom from an "offshore" perspective;

Mom and Dad for their valued support in spite of being plot characters;

Leanne for her usual unconditional support;

Lara for making it all worthwhile;

Jacquie (who skilfully danced upon the fine line between editor and co-author) for her slick, pro-active editing and unflagging belief in the project;

And especially Miche, for love and belief in me throughout, particularly in the very beginning – you made it happen!

FOREWORD

A Branch of Wisdom is an adventure of body, mind and spirit.

It plays with Logic and Intuition, with puns and coincidences, with time and perception.

The tale navigates a path between the turn of the millenium, and Christopher's life-shaping experiences as a white youth in the South Africa of the 1980s and 90s – a schizophrenic society where, at a socio-political level, in the oft-quoted words of WB Yeats: "Things fall apart. The centre cannot hold".

The author's quest is about finding that centring place of peace, tranquillity and meaning in the eye of the public and private storm. It is the individual's ongoing search for an *authentic* self.

The story traverses the South African border war. The alienated returning soldier experiences what western society constitutes as "breakdown". Despite prophecies of failure and future limitation, Christopher recovers in the eyes of the external world and does remarkably well in international finance. He is also accepted into the world of MENSA.

Then in his mid-30s, dogged by the black dog depression, he sets off on a search for understanding of his life thus far. So begins his philosophical quest – and the rebuilding of his life. He applies his fine intellect of head and heart as he follows the many forks of the Y shaped stick, first discovered in the psychiatrist's office. He traces this symbol through language theory to divining rods to the tree of life itself.

Christopher's quest twists and turns along many paths: Egyptian mythology, 17th century western philosophy and mathematics, Jungian psychology, eastern meditation, and the **I Ching**. Throughout, he ponders the meaning of the vision of two bodies levitating head to toe – one black, one white. He wonders what exists beyond the five senses of perception.

Christopher establishes hidden links between what appear to be separate worlds of west and east, inner and outer. This is the essence of metaphor – holding contradictions between unalikes, that reveal themselves anew in a flash of identity and shared purpose. The book is alive with such insights – revealing glimpses of how things are connected at deeper levels.

In this book Christopher walks the fine line between autobiography and fiction. Episodes such as his time in a mental hospital, and his visit to the east where he encounters the enigmatic Sam of the "Wisdom Shoppe", are particularly memorable. The writing is detailed, descriptive, nuanced, and often ironic and whimsical.

The text is accompanied by a website which features an innovative and conceptually brilliant array of metaphors for what could be described as visual puns. Christopher presents a playful interaction between contradictory states. And in so doing he challenges a society where an either/or paradigm holds on for grim life.

Richard Tarnas, author of The **Passion of the Western Mind**, discusses a dialectic in which "something from the past and something from the present come together and create the future. Two opposites converge to create a higher synthesis". This is the nature of this book. I trust that you will enjoy its challenges and disclosures as I have.

Dr Dorian Haarhoff
June 2002

Dorian Haarhoff is a well known South African author and poet, and former Professor of English Literature at the University of Namibia.

Sometime in your life you will go on a journey.
It will be the longest journey you have ever taken.
It is the journey to find yourself.

Katherine Sharp

What follows is based on the truth.

part I

WHAT HAPPENED

what happened

1984

The lesson is this: Your life tells you your path if you stop to look at the clues it has been throwing at you all of this time.

Geri Larkin

Premonition

"I could get out of this goddamned army in no time if I really wanted to!" Having said not a word for over half an hour, I found myself blurting it out, loudly and with an energy that startled the others. The words seemed to hang in the air, reverberating in the eerie silence that came over Driver's Platoon that Wednesday morning in 1984.

It was a sweltering hot Durban day. Our thick brown uniforms were prickly with sweat. A few of us drivers were sitting in a workshop, chatting idly to while away the tedium. We were all in the same long-term predicament, serving our two-year term with the South African Defence Force (SADF). In those early days of the 1980s the apartheid government was still in power and conscription was compulsory for all white males.

I hadn't been paying much attention to the conversation; the seven or eight whiskies I'd drunk the night before were producing a midday lethargy that tended to detach me a little. Ever since I'd wangled the transfer back to my hometown, my evenings had been one long string of booze-drenched parties. Back in the land of the living. Something to be cherished after the long months on the Border.

There were four of us in the workshop by the lorry park. At the back of the camp, it was off the main warpaths of the various Sergeants and Lieutenants who circulated during the day. Although it was somewhat musty and derelict, it was one of the better places to pass the time.

Ian and Dave had been debating how easy it would be to wangle a discharge from further military duty.
"I'm telling you bru, you just pretend you've gone *bossies*[1] and they won't want you anywhere near a rifle!" Dave enthused.
"Not so easy bru, they've got tests and things. Full-on psychologists and shit, bru." Ian – always the sceptic.

---

[1] 1980s SADF slang for "mad".

Rumours were always circulating about conscripts who had pretended so convincingly that they'd gone mad, they had received their discharges. How true these stories were, you could never tell. I hadn't personally witnessed a case, but legends as persistent as these would usually have a seed of truth in them somewhere, wouldn't they?

"Even if you could pull it off," Ian argued, "it wouldn't be worth it, bru. What you gonna do when you get onto Civvie Street and you've got a certificate that says you're *bossies*? How you gonna get a graft?"

It was at that point that I had made my single contribution to the conversation. But other than that outburst, that seemed to come inexplicably out of nowhere, it had been a week like any other in Natal Command. In retrospect, I would identify this as my first coincidence; not particularly significant, but a coincidence nevertheless. But at the time it happened nobody even saw it for what it was. And there were no further signs to suggest what was about to unfold.

The Calling

The second coincidence occurred around 5.30pm that Friday, as I was riding home for the weekend on a friend's motorbike. The bottlestore was due to close and I needed to get drinks for the party we were planning that evening, so I took a shortcut through the Muslim quarter of town. A large black BMW in front of me was holding me up and when a gap appeared momentarily in the traffic, I powered the throttle of the bike to overtake.

Suddenly, out of nowhere, emanated a blood-curdling wail – loud, haunting, and with a strangely primeval quality. It seemed to be directed *at me* and as it persisted, goosebumps broke out on my flesh. A strange sensation. Something stirring deep within me. Time frozen for the moment. I became aware that the wail was a man's voice. He had seen me coming. He had been waiting for me. My entire being resonated with the yell and I was, for an instant, suspended, in a trance. I had never experienced anything like it.

A sharp hoot from the BM snapped me back to the traffic and, as quickly as it had come, the sensation passed. I felt dazed and, clasping tightly onto the handlebars, swung into the slow lane. Only then did I notice the green and white minaret of the mosque beside the road, with its loudspeakers jutting out, the Muezzin summoning the faithful to evening prayers. I felt a little foolish, but I couldn't help noticing the coincidental timing of the whole thing. Almost as if somebody had "seen me coming".

By 8 o'clock that evening a few friends and I were sitting on the verandah of my parent's house, sipping drinks and puffing a pre-party joint. My parents were out for the evening and we'd agreed to meet there before driving into town. I used to smoke dope quite heavily in high school but had cut back a lot in the army. I preferred a good whisky these days.

The others were all very upbeat, but for some reason I was just not feeling myself that night. The whisky and dope didn't seem to be helping, and neither did the music that was playing in the background. The others hadn't seemed to notice though, so I laughed and joked along with them; I didn't want to be the party-pooper!

I took a second puff on the joint and sat back, watching the smoke rise in white mushroom clouds from my lungs. It was a beautiful evening. There were no clouds, and millions of stars sparkled in the deep blue sky. From the verandah you could see the sprawl of lights that was Durban and, beyond that, the purple ink of the night sea, with the twinkling light of a trawler or a cargo ship here and there. Summer was drawing to a close and there was the first hint of coolness in the air. Somewhere across the valley, a fiery-necked nightjar sent out into the night its characteristic call: "Good Lord Deliver Us".

My parent's house was a typically suburban, upper class white South African abode: five bedrooms, double garage and an acre of well-tended garden. From where we sat we looked over the glowing turquoise swimming pool, a Creepy-Crawly working its way systematically around the walls.

It took a while before I became aware that I was feeling more stoned than I should have been. I was only on my second whisky and had barely had two puffs of a joint. Nothing, compared to what I could normally handle. And yet I felt really spaced out. Something was bugging me but I couldn't pinpoint what. The others carried on talking and joking…

Then suddenly I realised what it was – the words of the song playing in the background! It was one of the New Romantic groups, "Naked Eyes", and the song was "Voices in my head". It had a very repetitive chorus and, without my realising it, the words "voices in my head" had been echoing around *in my head* for nearly two minutes now. I shuddered – it reminded me of the wail I'd heard earlier. This was the *last* song I needed tonight.

By the time we got into the car to drive into town, that sensation I'd had outside the mosque was back. I hadn't said a word for nearly half an hour. The others were beginning to notice; I saw concern in their fleeting glances at me and then back at one another.

When we arrived at the party, the feeling of being "out of it" was much worse. I could hardly move a muscle when the others all got out the car. I keeled over and lay on the back seat. "Hey, don't worry man, it happens to all of us," one of my friends laughed. He drove me back home so he could fetch his own car. He left me lying on the back seat of my car in the velvety darkness of my parent's driveway.

Double Vision

I'm not sure exactly what happened to me after that and I'm not sure that I ever will. It was a turning point in my life, so pivotal that it tends to divide my life into "everything before", and "everything after" – like BC and AD.

I listened to my friend's car reversing up the driveway and then driving up the road until I couldn't hear it anymore. Then there was silence…

Total silence. Total darkness too, as the streetlight was blocked by trees overhanging the car. The only thing I was aware of was the beating of my heart. I must have lain like that for minutes.

All at once I was engulfed by a tingling sensation and became aware of an image before me. It was vague at first, but gradually I made out the shape of two bodies lying in a sort of head to toe position with each other. The one seemed to be black and the other white. I sensed that they were both very important people. It was a feeling, more than an image – the words "ecstasy", "exhilaration", and "awe" come to mind, but they are inadequate to describe the feeling.

The uncanniest thing is that these two "personages" seemed familiar; only when the exhilaration became almost unbearably intense did I realise that I was looking at *myself*! Somehow I had detached from my body and was now suspended above the car, looking down on the body in the back seat. Except there were two of me – a black self and a white self. I felt at that moment that I was connected to the whole universe and the whole universe was connected to me, through my mind, which throbbed with a dull, pleasurable ache.

I'm not sure how long the experience lasted. At some point, I remember vaguely, I got out of the car and stumbled, as if sleepwalking, down the stairs, into the house, and into bed.

When I opened my eyes the next morning, the world was a new place.

My experience the night before had awakened, it seemed, a new faculty of vision within me and I felt as a blind man must feel when he sees for the first time. I saw deeper meanings in everything around me and felt that I suddenly understood the secret interconnectedness of the universe. I saw that the world I'd lived in my whole life thus far was a deceitful place, that the real truth lay hidden beneath the surface appearances. And I was aware that I too had been wandering around in an ignorant slumber. I felt like I'd been battling endlessly with some sacred cosmic puzzle and now, in an instant, I had caught sight of how it all fitted together.

I rushed upstairs to share my wonderful news with my parents. "The world is wrong," I told them excitedly. "Can't you see, it's all a big lie!" But from the outset it was evident that neither my mom, nor my dad, shared my enthusiasm. They greeted my outburst with puzzled responses. I tried my utmost to share with them what I could see, but the more I tried the more I realised how completely they had been deceived by the falsity of the world around them. They exchanged worried glances. Eventually, I had no option but to retreat to my room where I contemplated all that had happened to me the previous twelve hours.

I still wasn't exactly sure what the "vision" I had experienced the night before was all about. One thing I knew – it could not have been of this world. I didn't know where to turn, as I'd never really been spiritual or religious, despite having been brought up in our strictly Christian, white South African society.

I suppose it was this Christian upbringing that led me to the Bible. I had an old one at the back of my bookcase and I now seized it with fresh anticipation. I turned to Revelations, as that somehow seemed to me to be the right place to start. Skimming the musty pages, I searched for anything that might give me guidance about this new state that I had entered. I found it, everywhere:

> *If you have ears then listen to what the spirit says to the Churches.*

The same verse, again and again. It seemed significant because I had heard the voices in my head the day before. Now I realised that I was the one who had the ears! The more I read, the more things slotted into place. With growing awe I became aware that the Bible was speaking directly to me. I had been chosen – chosen by God to fulfil a very special mission. The vision I'd seen, I reasoned, had been sent directly from God. It was my calling to the holy cause.

I suppose it was only a matter of time before I would stumble across Revelations 13:18:

> *This calls for wisdom: let him who has understanding reckon the number of the beast, for it is a human number, its number is six hundred and sixty-six.*

666 – the number of the beast! It's hard to believe now, the power it had to strike fear into the heart of the average white South African. But if I think back to the apartheid South Africa of my youth, it was a fertile breeding ground for white paranoia! Rigid separation of white from black. Symbiotic relationship between Church and State (the Scriptures of an all-white God were used to justify the political rhetoric and actions of the ruling Afrikaners). Strict censorship. Draconian Pass Laws. Forced removals. A sophisticated machinery of control. All the violence and oppression necessary to prop up the system of white privilege. Everyone, in our close-knit, relatively conservative Christian community, felt the fear, even if we resisted it.

Constant rumours of Communist plots to overthrow the government. Frightened references to "*die Swart Gevaar*" (the black peril). Hushed discussions of the danger to white women posed by black men (or "native boys" as they were more commonly termed). Whispers about the evils of drugs and their relationship with "Devil-worshippers" or Satanists, bent on taking control. Fears of the coming of the anti-Christ and the end of the world.

I'd heard theories about how the barcodes on all South African products always start with a 6, have a 6 in the middle, and end with a 6. Now, in my newly heightened state of sensitivity and awareness, for the first time it dawned on me that the whispers and rumours might be true. Only a few weeks before I'd heard the theory that if you added up all the numbers on a roulette wheel, you would get the devil's number. At the time I had shaken my head, dismissing it with a snigger as yet more wild speculation by naïve people. But now, in my new frame of mind, I decided to verify the trickery for myself. I grabbed a calculator and punched in the numbers: 1 + 2 + 3 +… By the time I'd punched in 36, (the last digit) and saw the great big 666 flash up on the electronic display, my heart was pounding.

Seeing the Light

Monday morning arrived to find me still reeling from the weekend's discoveries. I could barely drag myself out of bed. On the way into camp I stopped and picked up my friend, James, and together we made the twenty minute drive into town. I hadn't left my room the whole weekend and now, for the first time, I was seeing Durban through new eyes. Evil was *everywhere*! In the newspaper headlines being peddled at the traffic intersections. On the bumper stickers of the passing cars. In the subtle comments of the morning DJs on the radio. And the most amazing thing was that nobody else seemed able to see it. I tried cautiously to test if James was noticing what was going on in the world, but I had to conclude that he too had been "contaminated with the blindness".

The evil I saw on that drive into town was a lot worse than I had anticipated and I reasoned to myself that my immediate priority was to find somebody who knew what was going on. There were huge stakes involved here and I didn't have any time to lose. I racked my brains for somebody I could turn to and finally thought of a possible ally: Roger Whitehead. He was a Christian minister and worked at a drug rehabilitation centre in town. (My parents had forced me to visit him in my high school days when they had first discovered that I smoked dope.) He'd always seemed a wise person to me.

When we got to the camp I told James, "I'm not coming in to army today". He stared at me, astonished, not sure if I was joking or not. When he saw I was serious he shrugged, "Hey, it's *your* funeral, bru".

It took me about ten minutes to get to Roger Whitehead's offices. I parked the car outside and strode confidently in the front door. Inside, I caught sight of some posters on the walls and a pang of terror struck me. Roger Whitehead had been hoodwinked too! The posters were so blatantly evil it was horrifying. "This can't be real," I told myself, "this can't be happening!"

The moment Whitehead came through to greet me I knew that my worst fears were confirmed. On his face he had that same bewildered expression that I was getting used to. "Can't you see the evil? Can't you see the evil?" I pointed excitedly at the posters.

He seemed alarmed and urged me to sit down in a rickety chair. He looked me up and down like it was the first time he had ever seen an army uniform and then he said: "Have you gone AWOL?" He said it slowly, pronouncing each letter one at a time. He was right, of course; technically I was Away Without Official Leave, but at that moment I had much more important responsibilities weighing upon me.

After a short conversation, he told me he wanted me to see somebody else and I followed him to another wing of buildings, to the office of a short, nervous looking man in a safari suit. He and Whitehead exchanged anxious sounding words behind closed doors. And then the short man asked me to explain to him slowly why I was there.

When I told him my story, he seemed to become even more anxious. He and Whitehead had another private conversation and then Whitehead asked me to follow him to his car. "Where are we going now?" I asked.
"I'm taking you back to the army camp," he said.
"What good is that going to do?" I protested.
"You will be safer there," replied Whitehead. And I figured that, in a strange kind of way, this made sense; I was, after all, valuable property, and maybe the army could offer me better protection from the forces of evil that had invaded society. "At least they have realised how important I am," I thought with some relief.

At about 11am Whitehead and I drove in his rusty Datsun through the main gates of Natal Command. We went directly to the sickbay, where Whitehead had some private words with the Lieutenant on duty. A nursing sister approached me and beckoned for me to come and sit in the shade. "No! I have seen the light," I protested.

When Whitehead left, I spent the afternoon preaching my testimony to the two nursing sisters and a Lance Corporal. "Open your ears and listen for the Spirit… If you've ever played roulette you must bet on zero, otherwise you'll be counted in the army of the Anti-Christ."

The Lance Corporal pointed out that the zero on the roulette wheel was how the casino made money, to which I replied, "Exactly! Do you think it's all just a big coincidence? I am the One shouting in the desert and you must listen for the Spirit, because it is always loudest in the desert. Everywhere else there are stones, and that's why you're all wandering around in such a stoned state".

They greeted my sermon with awe and fascination, it seemed to me. It was written all over their faces. It made perfect sense of course, as I was aware that it's not every day that you get to meet divinely chosen personages! Some excitement was to be expected.

That evening, my mother and father came to visit, trailing behind them a sheepish looking minister. "Aha!" I thought, "they've obviously had the good sense finally to wake up and take my weekend revelations seriously". But I soon gathered that the minister was as blind as everybody else was. I knew then that I was going to have to fight this battle on my own.

Outside the small window, shining through the evening haze, was a hotel sign: "Blue Waters". But the neon letters were white. I marvelled at the profoundness of this contradiction and pointed it out to the minister and my parents. "You see that light – it's actually white!" They couldn't seem to grasp the significance of it and I realised once again that it was only I who had the vision to see the secrets of the universe. Only I had seen the light.

Personal Greetings and Final Instructions

The next morning the Lieutenant told me to pack my belongings as I was being transferred to Addington Hospital on the beachfront.
"Hospital? Why a hospital?" I asked incredulously.
"They need to do some tests on you."

Once again it made perfect sense. "After all," my feverish reasoning went, "this is probably going to pan out to be the greatest scientific and religious discovery of the past few centuries!" I packed my bag, eager to co-operate.

MAN IC

MANTIC

MANTIC

MANTIC

©

"... manic excitement is a circumscribed psychotic episode of elation ... usually with grandiose delusions ..."
Encyclopedia Britannica

"mantic – divinatory personage who operates by the intervention of a spiritual power"
Encyclopedia Britannica

We drove along the beachfront, with buildings on one side and the ocean on the other. Small waves crashed softly on the golden beach. A light salt haze hung in the air and long tentacles of solid sunlight shafted between the tall buildings. I felt exhilarated. I could see and feel the divinity present all around me. This was *real*! It was really, really happening. God had chosen me. Life was full of meaning.

As we walked into the hospital foyer I noticed crowds of people milling around. Excitement rippled among them and I had a sneaking thought: "What if news has leaked out about my imminent arrival? Maybe I'll have to make a speech or something…"

But the Lieutenant just pushed me through the crowds and we went up to the 2nd floor. There, a woman was waiting for me. Dressed like a hippie, she rose to meet me, saying, "You're just a little boy trying to be brave". I reached hurriedly into my pocket for the miniature Bible that I now carried, but the Lieutenant pulled me away and ushered me into a small room with a hospital bed in the middle. Then he left, and I was alone.

It was the first time I had been alone for some time. I paced the small room. Then I stopped. Something strange was happening. That magical feeling I'd experienced on the drive along the beachfront was intensifying and my whole being began to tingle with excitement. It was a feeling not dissimilar to what I had felt in the back seat of the car that night; like a presence was in the room with me. A powerful yet benevolent presence…

I had a strong urge to write. Emptying out my bag, I grabbed a pad of paper and a pen. With surprising clarity, I drew a straight line down the middle of the page. Then I wrote the words that came to me – two lists of words, one on either side:

ADAM	EVE
DAY	NIGHT
DOG	CAT
WHITE	BLACK
POSITIVE	NEGATIVE

I placed the page in the centre of the bed so that the line in the middle of the page seemed to dissect the bed perfectly. Then I seized an orange plastic rubbish bin from the corner of the room and placed it at the foot of the bed in line with the dissecting line. On the bedside table lay a TV magazine with Tom Selleck on the cover. I rolled it up and placed it in the rubbish bin so that his moustached face peered out into the room from the top of the bin. Then I yanked off my army boots, and placed one on either side of the bin. I did this all with great energy and purpose. I felt that I was being guided by something. Or Someone.

It was then that I heard voices and I turned to see a tall brunette entering the room. Her hair was long and straight and she wore an oversized black shirt, untucked and hanging to her thighs. Clutched under her right arm was a large book and I caught a glimpse of the cover. **Chinese Philosophy and**… the title said.

She walked up and stood in front of the bed, reading the page that was placed in the middle. She observed the bin with my boots on either side. She knew. She didn't even have to look at me, I just knew that she knew. An air of peace and tranquillity seemed to radiate from her and I felt powerless in its force field.

But no sooner had she arrived than she disappeared, and I heard the voices resume. One was hers and the other a man's. They seemed to be arguing and I strained to catch their words. "…He's trying to tell us something – can't you see that…" But then a door closed and she was gone.

A few minutes later, and I was visited by a bespectacled man with a clipboard. He greeted me formally and then proceeded to take my temperature and blood pressure. He drew two huge test tubes of blood from me and then approached me with a large syringe full of green coloured liquid.

"Why the injection?" It was one thing taking blood from me (I had expected nothing less) but why would they want to inject anything *into* me?
"We need to calm you. It's critical for your state of health." His voice was as clinical as his face.
"And if I don't agree to the injection?"
He carried on rolling up my sleeve in order to find some suitable flesh. "It's always advisable to co-operate…"
Something in his tone suggested to me that I should co-operate and seconds later I felt a sharp bee sting in my shoulder.

My memories become jumbled after that. And from then on, the pills and injections never stopped but continued in an unrelenting and escalating barrage. There are plenty of memory fragments, but no time flow to hold them together in any kind of orderly fashion.

I recall looking all over the ward for the woman in black. I never found her. One afternoon when I was at the end of the corridor I saw a woman standing with her back to me talking on one of the payphones and I thought it might be her. She had the same long, dark hair and was talking excitedly on the phone in a foreign language. I figured that she was liaising with some top government official, maybe even in China; I was glad she was part of my team!

When the drug induced confusion first started, I turned to the Bible for clarity and guidance. For if God wanted me to save the world, as I was convinced he did, he was going to have to help me do it. This was now about international politics and God and the devil. I therefore gave God a type of ultimatum. It was the first evening that I was in hospital and I was alone by my bed.

"Dear God. I am going to take this Bible in my hand and open it. I implore You to guide me to the page You want me to read. I implore You to speak to me..."

The first words I read sent a cold shiver down my spine:

PERSONAL GREETINGS FINAL INSTRUCTIONS

God had spoken! To this day my stomach tightens when I recall those words. They weren't a hallucination – the words are still there on page 325 of my pocket Bible.

I went to bed that night with renewed zeal. There was absolutely no way that I could ignore this calling.

The Alpha and the Omega

I was not the only one inhabiting my ward. There were others too and we shared meals at a large communal dining room table. At first I wasn't sure how they fitted into the scheme of things. It had become clear to me that the bespectacled man in the white coat who administered the injections was quite high up in the chain of command in relation to my case, but he didn't always tell me what was going on. The presence of "others" therefore puzzled me but I figured that it was just part of the "testing". Some of the personnel were not convinced that I was who I said I was. So, these others were spies sent in to live with me in order to ascertain my authenticity. You couldn't blame them for testing me so thoroughly. The stakes involved in this whole thing were high and there was no room for error.

The guy in the room next to mine was Jewish and he came and talked to me a lot. He said he was in advertising but it didn't take me long to work out that he was actually a high ranking Rabbi

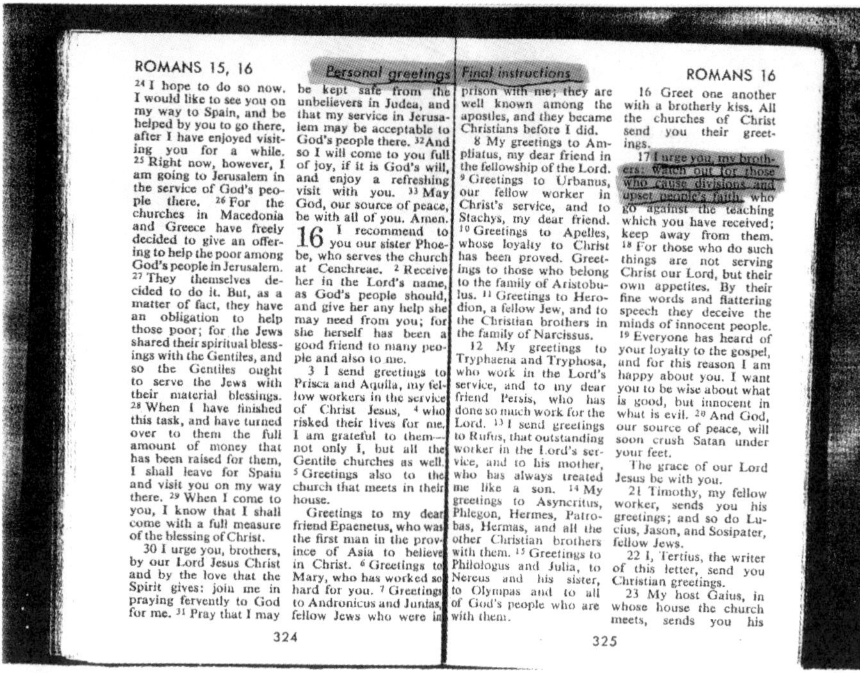

ROMANS 15, 16

24 I hope to do so now. I would like to see you on my way to Spain, and be helped by you to go there, after I have enjoyed visiting you for a while. 25 Right now, however, I am going to Jerusalem in the service of God's people there. 26 For the churches in Macedonia and Greece have freely decided to give an offering to help the poor among God's people in Jerusalem. 27 They themselves decided to do it. But, as a matter of fact, they have an obligation to help those poor; for the Jews shared their spiritual blessings with the Gentiles, and so the Gentiles ought to serve the Jews with their material blessings. 28 When I have finished this task, and have turned over to them the full amount of money that has been raised for them, I shall leave for Spain and visit you on my way there. 29 When I come to you, I know that I shall come with a full measure of the blessing of Christ.

30 I urge you, brothers, by our Lord Jesus Christ and by the love that the Spirit gives: join me in praying fervently to God for me. 31 Pray that I may

Personal greetings

be kept safe from the unbelievers in Judea, and that my service in Jerusalem may be acceptable to God's people there. 32 And so I will come to you full of joy, if it is God's will, and enjoy a refreshing visit with you. 33 May God, our source of peace, be with all of you. Amen.

16 I recommend to you our sister Phoebe, who serves the church at Cenchreae. 2 Receive her in the Lord's name, as God's people should, and give her any help she may need from you; for she herself has been a good friend to many people and also to me.

3 I send greetings to Prisca and Aquila, my fellow workers in the service of Christ Jesus, 4 who risked their lives for me. I am grateful to them—not only I, but all the Gentile churches as well. 5 Greetings also to the church that meets in their house.

Greetings to my dear friend Epaenetus, who was the first man in the province of Asia to believe in Christ. 6 Greetings to Mary, who has worked so hard for you. 7 Greetings to Andronicus and Junias, fellow Jews who were in

324

Final instructions

ROMANS 16

prison with me; they are well known among the apostles, and they became Christians before I did.

8 My greetings to Ampliatus, my dear friend in the fellowship of the Lord. 9 Greetings to Urbanus, our fellow worker in Christ's service, and to Stachys, my dear friend. 10 Greetings to Apelles, whose loyalty to Christ has been proved. Greetings to those who belong to the family of Aristobulus. 11 Greetings to Herodion, a fellow Jew, and to the Christian brothers in the family of Narcissus.

12 My greetings to Tryphaena and Tryphosa, who work in the Lord's service, and to my dear friend Persis, who has done so much work for the Lord. 13 I send greetings to Rufus, that outstanding worker in the Lord's service, and to his mother, who has always treated me like a son. 14 My greetings to Asyncritus, Phlegon, Hermes, Patrobas, Hermas, and all the other Christian brothers with them. 15 Greetings to Philologus and Julia, to Nereus and his sister, to Olympas and to all of God's people who are with them.

16 Greet one another with a brotherly kiss. All the churches of Christ send you their greetings.

17 I urge you, my brothers: Watch out for those who cause divisions and upset people's faith, who go against the teaching which you have received; keep away from them. 18 For those who do such things are not serving Christ our Lord, but their own appetites. By their fine words and flattering speech they deceive the minds of innocent people. 19 Everyone has heard of your loyalty to the gospel, and for this reason I am happy about you. I want you to be wise about what is good, but innocent in what is evil. 20 And God, our source of peace, will soon crush Satan under your feet.

The grace of our Lord Jesus be with you.

21 Timothy, my fellow worker, sends you his greetings; and so do Lucius, Jason, and Sosipater, fellow Jews.

22 I, Tertius, the writer of this letter, send you Christian greetings.

23 My host Gaius, in whose house the church meets, sends you his

325

Photocopy of page 325 of the American Bible Society's **The New Testament** – the page that I opened on 8 March 1984, after asking God for a message.

from Israel. Probably posted by the Jews to keep the Holy Land up to date on the latest developments. There was a small TV in the ward and I had seen on the news that there was something big happening in Israel – bloody protests, people chanting, fires and bombs. I was amazed to see that my presence had thrown such a cat amongst the pigeons.

Then I discovered a collaborator. A large glass fish-tank had also infiltrated the ward, occupying a space against the wall in the TV room. I didn't notice it at first, but one morning as I walked past I became aware of one of the fish looking at me. In an instant I realised that this fish knew too. I spent many hours, after that, peering into the miniature world of fish; it was so obvious that they knew what was going on, that I couldn't believe that nobody else had ever noticed. The one that knew the most was a small, white fish that used to keep to itself most of the time. Not only did it know about me, but it also *believed* in me. The others all seemed to know too (I could see by the way they looked at me), but it was apparent that they didn't all share the same faith in me. In fact, as the days went by, I became aware that a large black dogfish had aligned with the forces of Darkness and was just waiting for the right opportunity to pounce on the faithful one and possibly end its life. The faithful one knew too, because it kept its distance from the evil one, and was visibly nervous most of the time.

One evening, still amazed at the Personal Greeting I had received from God, I decided to look back at those mystical biblical pages which had revealed the message to see if there were any further instructions. I read every word on page 325 but could not really glean much that seemed pertinent. There was only one verse that made any sense and even that I wasn't quite clear about. Romans 14:13:

> *I urge you my brothers, watch out for those who cause divisions and upset people's faith.*

I couldn't quite put my finger on it, but somewhere deep within I had a strong feeling that these were the words that were meant for my Mission.

Elsewhere in the great book other words seemed to beckon to me, especially in Revelations. It was God speaking, at the height of the Great War with the devil, and He kept saying:

I am the Alpha and the Omega.

Again, I didn't know why these words fascinated me so much. It took my dad to explain that the Alpha and the Omega were the first and last letters of the ancient Greek alphabet. Having used these symbols previously in some mathematical formula, he drew me a picture of each. The lower case of Alpha was:

$$\alpha$$

and of Omega:

$$\omega$$

I scribbled these symbols down on a journal page for safekeeping.

At the front of the ward, overlooking the sea, was a tiny room called "The Sun Room" and I went there during the day to sit and look out over the ocean. Strange puns occurred to me in that room; I remember waving one day at the sea and then realising that I was *waving* at the *waves*. And then it occurred to me that I could *see* the *sea*. And why was it called the Sun Room? Was it not the *Son's* room? There was some secret code hidden in all of this, no doubt about it. But I would crack it sooner or later. Wars always had passwords and codes, and this Great War, between God and the devil, was obviously no exception.

Other than the TV, which used to broadcast the news to the agents and me every evening, I had little contact with the outside world.

But it was apparent from TV coverage that something big was going down. Worried looking world leaders rushed back and forth to Israel. Iraqi jets battled over Iran. Then one business report spoke about “bonds”, “guilts” and “corporate prophets”. The Code again. They tried to make it look like it was all meant to be financial, but I wasn’t conned. The time was coming…

All the while the head doctor kept running tests, drawing syringes of blood, and scribbling notes on his clipboard. He was worried. “Clearly,” I figured to myself, with some compassion, “he has never had to deal with a case of such solemnity, and he is feeling out of his depth. And who could blame him? Phenomena like me don’t turn up every day”.

After about a week or so a new agent was introduced into the ward. He was younger than the rest, probably only a year or two older than me, with bad scars all the way up both arms. One morning he asked me to play a game of chess. I was wary but agreed, as chess is a game I have always loved. When we set up the pieces, I landed up with black, and he with white. I began to feel quite agitated; after all, this was a terrible way to start. Clearly I should not have been associated with the forces of Darkness. Had it not been for an odd coincidence I wouldn't have worried so much; one of the black bishops was missing and in its place was a *red* plastic bishop that must have come from another set. So not only was I commandeering the forces of Darkness, but I also had an infiltrator in my ranks: a red Communist that had ousted one of my holy bishops, and taken its position between the queen and the knight (*the knight of the night* – that diabolical Code again).

But it was too late to back out and I braced myself for the opening move. For the first few minutes we felt each other out around the board. I kept my eye at all times on the red bishop, aware that he was not to be trusted. After about twenty minutes a few pawns were gone and a knight each, but nobody really had the upper hand. A few other agents had gathered around the table and were watching with interest. Then, in a matter of moments, things began to change. I put the white king into check with my rook. The king moved out of danger to a square to the left. That's when I saw the checkmate. In an instant I saw that if I moved the red bishop two spaces forward to the left, the white king was trapped and had to admit defeat.

I sat there staring at the pieces for a long time after the game. Why had it been the Communist that had killed the white king? Of all the possible outcomes, why had fate chosen the *impostor*? How had the game turned out that way? I certainly hadn't planned it, so who had? I felt spooked.

Ward 24

It must have been after I'd been there about eleven days that the Welfare Lieutenant from Natal Command arrived at the hospital. He bore important news. "Addington has informed us that they are no longer sufficiently equipped to handle your case. On Sunday you're going to be transferred to 1 Military Hospital in Pretoria which can offer you far better treatment."

I wasn't entirely happy with the decision, as I had grown to like my new home. But after some consideration I deduced that it might be better to be stationed in a military hospital when the final Great War broke out as there were bound to be skirmishes. Addington was not adequately defended.

The day before the transfer the chess player and I were allowed a short walk on the beach and we scuttled across the sand in our "technicolour dream-coats" like two giant crabs. Having not been out of doors since my admission, I blinked in the bright sunlight. We made our way down to the sea and there I waved my final goodbyes to the waves. People sitting on the beach stared at us, fascinated by our attire, but it didn't worry me. In a way I felt sorry for them; it was obvious they didn't have a clue about the War and what was coming.

At the last minute the military agreed to let my mother and father drive me to Pretoria and I figured that it was probably to throw the enemy off guard. "A clever move," I reasoned to myself, "we did that in Angola once – planned the whole trip in *Ratels* and then switched over to *Buffels* on the actual morning". Before we left, the doctor handed me a large brown envelope. On the cover were the words: "Paranoid Schizophrenia". I had heard this term somewhere before but decided that it must be a military code name for my special case. These damned Codes!

The drive from Durban to Pretoria seemed to last forever. They had given me extra injections that morning, and I spent most of the time lying on the backseat. Every now and then I'd surface, and look through the windows to see where we were. At one point I heard a helicopter overhead and wondered if my parents were aware that we were being secretly escorted by the military. By the time we got to the outskirts of Pretoria, there were military vehicles everywhere; there was a stage when we had one in front and one behind. No doubt about it – an officially organised convoy.

The hospital was a vast square building jutting into the sky like a slab of granite. Inside, it was spotlessly clean. Glistening floors and walls. A stench of disinfectant. And uniformed medics rushing around throwing salutes. After "checking in" at the main lobby, we were told to follow an ambulance in our car, to another military building about three kilometres away. It was dark by the time we arrived but I could see that this was much older than the main hospital, with a dilapidated facade.

A Captain greeted us. I was taken down a long corridor to a door with the words "Ward 24" written above it. Inside, the doors opened up onto a large open-plan hallway with long rows of military beds lining both walls. Soldiers were scattered around the ward smoking, playing cards and watching TV. Most of them wore dream-coats, but I could see that they were soldiers. They didn't take much notice of me as I walked in. Obviously they had not been warned about my arrival. Maybe it was a good thing. If the military thought it best to downplay the whole thing, so would I.

After my parents left, two burly male nurses arrived and took four test tubes of blood from me. By now I had great purple bruises all the way up both arms from all the blood tests. What were they doing with all my blood? Probably sending it to the USA and Israel. After all, this was a world event.

In the middle of the hall a row of three tables was joined together, with chairs pulled up on either side. I could see the remains of the evening's supper on the tablecloth. A verandah adjoined the ward on one side, with a ping-pong table at one end and a small TV at the other. Two soldiers played ping-pong and a few others watched TV. Behind the ping-pong table a glass door opened onto what looked like a small garden. A glass cubicle commandeered the head of the ward and inside sat a surly looking Private in full uniform. He peered out at us through the cubicle windows and seemed every now and then to make notes in a large black book.

I buried myself in the Bible until the lights were switched out and most guys got into bed. Before long one or two snores started up, but it was evident that not everybody was sleeping. At the far end of the ward a thin, pale looking guy shuffled very slowly down the centre of the room. His arms didn't move, but remained stiff at his sides. His feet inched forward slowly, one foot at a time. His face was blank, his eye staring, unblinkingly, straight ahead. "A Shuffler!" I thought to myself, grinning inwardly at my nickname for the poor man.

A Prophet

I didn't sleep at all that night. My mind was pre-occupied with the War that was surely coming. Being back in a military environment had snapped me out of the dreamlike lull I had entered at Addington. Here there *was* a war going on. Even more disturbing was my growing suspicion as to the hidden meaning contained in the Biblical verse in Romans, "I urge you my brothers watch out for those who cause divisions and upset people's faith…" The division was apartheid, I was beginning to think. I had never agreed with apartheid. It had been one of the reasons I had rebelled against the whole establishment in high school. What if the Nationalist government was the one that was "causing divisions", and I was the brother being urged to take heed? What if I wasn't so safe after all, here in Pretoria, in the heart of the apartheid capital?

Grappling with this new suspicion, I went through a full packet of cigarettes that night. Once or twice a soldier screamed in his sleep, the sound ringing up and down the cold corridor like a nocturnal phantom. At times I paced about, and on one walkabout found a small kitchen next to the Private's glass cubicle. Inside, a microwave and a fridge. Rows and rows of test tubes containing blood lined the inside of the fridge door. Some of the blood must have been mine. I was aware of the cubicled Private's eyes on me as I paced. Every ten minutes or so he would scribble something in that book of his.

6am. The first glow of daylight seeped through from the verandah. My body felt tense. Soon a few soldiers stirred and then one or two jumped out of bed. A guy at the far end of the ward shouted for everybody to wake up, "Hurry, hurry… He's coming soon!" There seemed a hint of panic in the air and everybody scrambled out of bed. A state of high frenzy ensued as soldiers tidied their bedside tables and pulled their blankets and sheets straight. "He's coming! He's coming!"

One of the soldiers closest to the door shouted: "Attention!" and all the soldiers rushed to the foot of their beds and stood to attention in their dream-coats. I stood in line with them, sensing the fear in the air.

The staccato clip clop of army boots grew louder. Then a beefy Sergeant barged through the doors at the far end of the ward. He started inspecting each soldier's area, one by one. He had with him a large stick and he stopped at the bed of the Shuffler from the night before, who had somehow also managed to manoeuvre into position. “You fucking *moffie*!”, the Sergeant bellowed in his face, poking his stick viciously into the man’s stomach. “You cowards might be able to fucking fool the nurses but you can’t fucking fool me!” The Shuffler stared ahead, his face twitching uncontrollably.

Suddenly I was scared. I had been through hundreds of inspection parades before and I was used to the insults and bellowing. They had never phased me. But this time it was different. This Sergeant was evil. I had sensed his evil presence the moment he’d walked through the door. A terrifying realisation formed in my mind: *this Sergeant* was the enemy; *he* was the front guard of the forces of Darkness. And I knew that he knew I was here. For the first time I felt a tremor in my knees. When I tried to control it I couldn’t.

Slowly the Sergeant worked his way down the ward, one bed at a time. Now and then he’d stop and poke his stick in somebody’s stomach and scream and curse about *moffies*, cowards, hippies and drug addicts. 24 hours had passed since I’d left Addington and I had not had any medication. My shaking was getting worse. By the time the Sergeant turned the corner at my end of the ward and got to my bed, my knees were knocking against each other. In two strides the Sergeant reached my bed and stopped directly in front of me. His big red face loomed above me.

“Aha, a fucking newcomer!” he shrieked in my face. “And look what a fucking shambles his bed is! Look’s like a bloody whorehouse! Whose cunt are you going to fuck *soutie*, your mother’s?” He lifted his stick and I felt its butt strike me in the stomach and drive all the breath out of me. “I know why you’re here, *soutie*! I know exactly why you're here. But you can't escape from me!" He stood there staring down at me, his evil eyes drilling holes in my being. It must have been a full five minutes before he moved on.

When they brought breakfast about ten minutes later I had so much adrenaline pumping through my veins that I could hardly eat. Then we had to line up and I was given a handful of six different coloured pills and was watched as I swallowed them. There was no doubt in my mind now – the War had begun. Somehow Satan had managed to infiltrate his army into this very hospital.

Later that morning nurses came in and told us all to take a seat around the large tables. We were each given two pieces of paper and told to draw a picture on each piece. On the first piece we were to draw a picture of "how we were", and on the second "how we are now". "They're testing me again," I muttered to myself, through gritted teeth. "Clearly, the people in this place are not aware of who I really am."

As we sat there the feeling of being mesmerised started coming over me. Subtle at first, it gradually grew into the same feeling I'd experienced when I had first been admitted to hospital. I began feeling strong, invincible, like I had tuned into some higher, psychic power. But paradoxically I was also powerless in its presence. I was a feather caught in a strong wind.

The others had started drawing their pictures but I couldn't. The force seemed to take control of me. I stood up from my seat and walked very, very slowly around the table. I circled it in slow motion, three times. By the third, the eyes of the nurses and soldiers were following my every move. I glided towards the kitchen that I'd discovered the night before and, once there, opened the fridge. Grabbing a test tube of blood, I glided slowly back to the table.

By now there was total silence in the ward, everyone captivated by my actions. I sat down at my seat in front of the pieces of paper. I opened the test tube, stuck my finger in the blood, and wrote slowly with my bloodied finger:

I am, a
Prophet
signed
Christopher

Rainbow Nation

That morning's art session had a profound effect on my status in the ward. Pandemonium broke out shortly after I finished my artwork and the nurses couldn't cope. Two hefty male orderlies arrived and thrust a gigantic syringe into my backside. Things became vague and jumbled after that…

For the next few days people steered pretty clear of me. Occasionally one or two soldiers would come and whisper a few things to me but they would never stay long. A tall guy with John Lennon glasses came one day and sat opposite me. "You're a psychologist, bru, I can see it. I just hope for your sake that they don't see through you. Because I can, bru…" On another occasion, a short, dark haired guy with darting eyes, whispered: "Don't worry – you're not the only one. I've seen the evil too…There's a big computer in Belgium right now called 'The Beast' and every time you enter it you have to enter 666. …The Brotherhood of Ram… It's here…"

I was assigned to a woman psychiatrist and she spent long hours interviewing me. Hundreds of questions: about my past; about my sex life; about my family; about my time in Angola. I had expected this. In order to verify my status they needed all the information they could get, I thought to myself. She examined my head and stared into my pupils with a stethoscope. "You can look in my pupils," I told her, "but I am God's pupil. You can look at my temples but I am in God's temple". The Code.

From time to time new soldiers would arrive. Some of them would leave after a day or two. Others would stay. Two *Recces* arrived one day, apparently flown in straight from Angola. They spent their hours digging holes in the garden and then filling them up again. Their faces and bodies were a sunburnt chocolate brown and their eyes – their eyes were completely vacant. Two other Shufflers had joined the first Shuffler and they spent their days and nights slowly working their way from one end of the ward to the other – like a small flotilla of lost ships in the night. A squat guy with curly black hair ran around at random intervals, shouting "Ping Pong! Ping Pong!" at the top of his voice. On one occasion, another soldier, wearing a black bandanna, walked down one of the corridors, smashing every window as he went. Thirty-eight in total. The Private sat in the glass cubicle watching it all, scowling, and writing notes in his black book.

Satan's Sergeant came every morning, and every morning my shaking got worse. He never failed to stop in front of my bed and poke me in the stomach with his stick. "This is not fucking heaven, *soutie*, this is the fucking army!" One day two vicious German Shepherds accompanied him on his inspection, apparently to sniff out any *dagga*.[2] But one of the soldiers was so terrified of the dogs that he went into a type of epileptic fit and lay writhing on the floor, foam bubbling from his mouth. Four male orderlies had to hold him down to inject him. The Sergeant beamed from ear to ear.

I couldn't take it any more. I took a pen and scribbled a note.

The next time the Sergeant came I stuck the note out for him to take:

RE: WARD
There will be a REWARD
<u>A WARD</u>
AWARD to those who fought in <u>a</u> WAR <u>d</u>.
<u>A D</u>
Anno Domine
After Death
You can nail me to a cross if you like.

W
C R O S S
R
D
S

DEAD END.

---

[2] South African term for marijuana.

After that day, he never stopped in front of my bed again. But the shaking didn't go away.

At the top of the ward were some private cubicles. One was occupied by an artist. Why he had his own cubicle nobody knew. He spent his time sketching with dark leaded pencils – pictures of witches and wizards and frogs. Incredible pictures, lifelike and detailed. On nights when I couldn't sleep and paced around the ward, I would see the light burning in his cubicle, his mind absorbed in the sketching.

The only real friend I made was a little black cat that used to come and visit during the days. We seemed able to communicate with each other, the cat and I. Everybody was busy with their stupid things, but the cat and I were the only ones who really knew. Often soldiers would play Mastermind at the table in the middle of the ward, and every time the cat would curl up in the lid of the Mastermind box, and look out onto the world. *We* were masterminds, the cat and I.

All the while the Great War between good and evil continued raging. Things were not looking good for God's armies and I was beginning to fear the worst. But at least I was getting closer to cracking the Code. The letter S was my clue. It was an evil letter, I'd discovered: Serpents, Snakes, Sin, Satan and Six hundred and Sixty Six. The SSS.

It was also around this time that I made the terrifying discovery that all of the nurses, doctors and medics wore badges on their uniforms – the badge featured two serpents curled around a staff. For a long time I had not known whom I could trust and whom I couldn't. Of all of them, the female nurses had seemed to be the least likely to be in Satan's army. But now, with this discovery that even they wore serpents, I felt increasingly vulnerable.

The pills had increased to ten in the morning and four at lunch and supper. They clouded my mind and I battled to concentrate.

One morning, really frustrated, I went to the athletics field in the hospital grounds to take a jog. I'd been fit before this whole thing began and I figured that a run would clear my head. "Maybe I could even start running every day," I planned to myself. But I was in for a nasty shock. When I tried to run I found that I couldn't. My feet were blocks of lead and I just couldn't lift them fast enough. It was that terrible sensation you sometimes get in nightmares when you are running away from an attacker but seem to be held back by an invisible gravitational force. I began to realise what the snakes on the badges were for; they were slowly poisoning me.

On the way back to the ward, I made another startling discovery. I came upon an open courtyard and there I saw a terrible sight. Dozens of black soldiers milled about in dream-coats. What made it so eerie was that all of them had limbs missing. Some had smooth brown stumps at the knees, some at the elbows. The unluckiest ones had stumps at both knees and elbows.

That afternoon I made a special request to see the army Chaplain, and he came to my bed in the early evening. He was Afrikaans and dressed in a military uniform from head to toe. I showed him my Bible and told him about the personal greetings message. I explained, as best I could, that God had shown me that apartheid was evil, and wanted me to do something about it. I expressed my fears that they were slowly poisoning me. I'm not sure what I said wrong, but the Chaplain looked extremely confused and almost, I suspected, embarrassed.

"My friend you must be very, very careful," he said, ducking his head and looking around nervously. "God's enemies – the Communists and the blacks – they are very, very tricky. They have cast doubt into your mind and now you are imagining these things. That is their plan. Now, these good medical people here; they are in the service of your country and of God. Why would you doubt them?" He looked earnestly into my face, his expression puzzled. As he did so, he kept wringing his hands, which he held up at chest level. "They are simply trying to get you back from the devil, onto the right side of the fence." His voice got more animated, "Yes, they are shepherds looking after the volk. You see, the volk and the flock – we both go astray... And then we can thank *onse Vader* for sending guardians to watch over us". He said a quick prayer in Afrikaans, asking God to protect and guide me, and then he left. I never saw him again.

The sluggishness from the drugs intensified. Days went by and then weeks. Eventually, with horror I realised that I, too, had become a Shuffler. I could no longer swing my arms. They just hung, like solid steel pipes, at my sides. And my feet inched forward, half a foot at a time. It took me ages to get to the workshop on the days when we did remedial crafts. I was working on a wood burning. Trying to burn the letters of a quotation onto the wood. "IT'S BETTER TO BURN OUT THAN TO FADE AWAY". Wasn't sure where I had heard those words before. It seemed to be taking an immensely long time, burning out each letter into the wood. The poison was winning the battle.

One day, after I'd run out of money for cigarettes, one of the nurses accompanied me across the road. "I'll just take you across to the teller then, shall I, so you can get some money," she'd said. I wondered, "What kind of teller would I find. Is this a fortune teller; will she *tell* me my fortune? What will she charge? Will it *cost* me a fortune?" My mind was reeling with the connections and gaps that I heard in what people said. When we got there I gave the fortune teller my secret number and the fortune teller gave me some money and a small slip of paper. I looked at the paper. "So, not much of a fortune, after all," I said to the nurse. She smiled kindly at me, took my hand and guided me back across the road away from the automatic teller machine. I only had a few hundred Rand left in my account. That was my fortune. The whole thing was coded, like everything else. And was my fortune timed to run out when the Great War started, I wondered...

More soldiers came and went. One day they bought in a Lieutenant from the Parabats, who had lost two men in his platoon. He was given a special cubicle alongside the artist, and didn't have to stand inspection. He spent about three days wailing incessantly before he was released.

Along the way I was making incredible progress on my Mission. I drew a bold rainbow on the cover of my journal. The colours stood for all the people of South Africa, for it was going to be a Rainbow Nation. I told everybody about this, about the pot of gold at the end of the rainbow; "Undivided, my brothers," I said, but it fell on deaf ears.

God showed me astonishing things. I saw how the Great War was raging in the heavens. At night the Southern Cross protected the night sky. But if you looked closely on a clear night, you could see a black smudge below the Southern Cross and that was the Black Hole, the devil waiting to swallow us all up. Sometimes I would sing "Silent Night". Except, instead of "holy night", I would sing "holey night". Nobody understood. Only I had seen the light. Only I had heard the Code.

Then for a while God showed me threes. Everything came in threes: the three primary colours; past, present and future; positive, negative and zero; gases, solids and liquids; the Father, Son, and "Holey" Ghost. The Old Testament, the New Testament and me in between. Three sixes. Three, I concluded triumphantly, was the secret of the universe.

I had been grappling with the Greek Alpha and Omega for many weeks now. I knew that there was a secret locked up somewhere in that pair. For if God was the Alpha and the Omega, then God was somehow divinely captured in those symbols. One night I finally clicked: the Alpha and the Omega had to be joined.

psychotic©

I took the Alpha α and by rotating it ninety degrees and connecting it to the Omega ω I got this:

There I had it! God was one. I was one. It was late at night and the other soldiers were sleeping. To celebrate my discovery I took a wide tipped marker pen, and wrote in big black letters on the wall:

THE WRITING IS ON THE WALL

When they found the writing, they were really bothered. I don't know why, but they were.

Driftwood

On the second to last day I was sent to the far corner of the hospital where a very important man had an office. A professor of Psychiatry and Psychology, he was apparently one of the most learned men in his field in the Southern Hemisphere. I packed my journal for the long journey, anxious to show the professor my discoveries. He was my last ray of hope. Surely *he* would understand?

Before leaving the ward I stopped to admire the new drawing the artist was working on. It was a surreal picture, portraying a city constructed from what looked like giant anthills. There were little caves everywhere, all interlinked. In the middle was a vast pyramid that looked out of place in the rest of the picture. A lone lightning bolt reached down out of the sky and struck the apex of the pyramid. "Do you like it, brother?" He always called me brother. I told him that I did.

The journey to the professor's office was twisting and tortuous, and seemed to take hours. One of the female nurses led me by the hand down long, sterile passages with military people moving efficiently around. I could feel the panic in the air. Definitely a War. From time to time we came to enclaved waiting rooms and in these rooms were civilians as well as soldiers. I was exhausted that morning, and even shuffling seemed a terrible task. From time to time I would stop and lie down in the passage, curling up in little puddles of light from the windows. The nurse would plead with me to get up and follow her. "Please Chris, please. It's not far now, I promise you. We'll be there soon. Just a little longer…" People walking past gave me a wide berth.

When we finally got to the professor's waiting room I curled up on a couch and waited my turn. An electrical socket in the wall caught my eye and I stared at its shape for a long time. Electricity also came in threes, I noted: positive, neutral and earth. The more I stared at the three circular holes in the wall the more I began to think that the socket was identical to the Alpha and the Omega that I had joined. It also consisted of three spheres. I could feel power coming out of that socket – vast invisible arms of secret energy that swirled around the room, transparently energised ghosts dancing in the air.

Finally a lady in a frumpy red dress indicated it was my turn. I entered the professor's elegant office and sat down opposite him, at a low coffee table. He was a fat man with beady eyes and a smug demeanor. His neck was non-existent, his head seeming like an extension of his upper torso. He observed me with an air of disdain, waiting for me to say something.

I opened my journal to where I had joined the Alpha and the Omega. "Look!" I said, "the Alpha and the Omega". He examined the picture for a while and then shook his head: "Look's like a penis to me". A silence ensued, during which I tried to fathom the import of what he had said.

It was at that moment that I caught sight of an unusual object on the table. It was a branch of driftwood, bleached and smooth from many years of wind and sun. It was symmetrically shaped in a perfect Y. Striking.

I reached forward and touched it, and as I did I felt a magical sensation come over me. It was the same feeling I had experienced now a few times before – that feeling of ecstatic revelation, as though God was there, in the room with us, touching my very soul; the whole universe connected to me, everything in its perfect place, everything crystallised in an eternal moment.

I sat like that, holding the magical branch, for what must have been a full five minutes. I was in a trance and I never wanted to let it go. Eventually the professor cleared his throat and started reading aloud from a file the nurse had handed him. I never really heard what he was reading – it seemed to be mainly medical jargon concerning the pills I was taking. After that he scribbled down some of his own notes, tried to make small talk, and shook my hand as I left his office.

666

When I got back to the ward that afternoon I saw that the artist had been busy all day on his picture. He had made a lot of progress on the lightning bolt, and now, instead of a lone bolt reaching down from the sky, there was a whole army of lightning bolts sizzling and forking and striking the apex of the pyramid. The picture had caused quite a stir among the soldiers and there was much speculation about what it might mean. The artist had named it "The Pict", and one soldier was saying that there was an ancient Celtic tribe that lived in caves in Britain called the Picts. That is why there were so many caves. "No," said another soldier, "the Pict is just short for Picture".

I didn't sleep that night. After supper I watched the 8 o'clock news. It was the first time in a long time that I'd seen what was going on in the outside world, and it wasn't good. War everywhere. Video clips of seething masses of angry Palestinians, burning flags and brandishing weapons. A bomb gone off in Northern Ireland. An Iraqi jet shot down by the Iranians. The war in Angola – still raging. Worried looking politicians racing around the world attending summits. People dying. Panic and mayhem everywhere. A total nightmare. The end was nigh…

That whole night my head spun with ideas, images, shapes. There were snakes and sixes and triples and doubles, crosses and black holes, and armoured cars driving into the red Angolan sunset. Codes and passwords. Devils flashed in and out too. But all the time the rainbow shone. And the pot of gold at the end of the rainbow was undivided, my brothers. The writing *was* on the wall. They had even left it there where I had scrawled it in big black letters, and still they couldn't see what it meant. Satan was close, there was no doubt about it. And *I* was the one who had to do something about it. *I* was the one who had been chosen – I was thc one who had been picked. Stupid soldiers – thinking the Pict stood for cave dwellers or pictures. It didn't stand for either. It stood for me: *The Picked*. Only the artist knew. And Satan.

I don't know how I arrived at the next conclusion but it had something to do with the Pict and the 8 o'clock news and the professor's office. My mind raged for hours and hours and then suddenly everything came together. It slotted into place. *I* was the Alpha and the Omega! *I* was God!

To this day I cannot adequately describe the feeling of totally believing, beyond a shadow of a doubt, that you are God. Not his son, not a messenger, not a prophet – but the one and only Creator of the entire universe! The real McCoy!

I should have known it was going to be a bad day when the sun finally started leaking through the glass doors on the other side of the ping-pong table. It was a great red sun. "Red sky in the morning, *Shepherd's Warning*." Already the sheep were beginning to run around and bleat. The Ping-Ponger was shouting "Ping Pong Ping Pong!" The Shufflers were shuffling and the clock was ticking. I could wait no longer.

I grabbed my Bible and shuffled as fast as I could down the passage to the officer on duty. He was a Captain of the Medical Corps and sat sternly at his desk, no doubt eager to be relieved of his shift. "You *have* to listen to me!" I shouted. "For your own good you have to listen to me!" He seemed alarmed and cowered behind the desk. I opened the Bible to John 14:30. I had highlighted the words with my glowing green highlighter during the night. At the top of my voice I read:

> *I cannot talk with you much longer, for the ruler of this world is coming. He has no power over me, but the world must know that I love the Father; that is why I do everything he commands me . . .*

I couldn't finish my words. Two aggressive male orderlies appeared out of nowhere and dragged me back to the ward where they plunged a gigantic syringe into me. Satan was here, he was fighting for his life.

Back at the ward there was more pandemonium. Soldiers were shouting in the bathrooms and nurses rushed back and forth. The injection had paralysed me and I couldn't get off my bed to see what was going on. But word got back to me; the little black cat had been found with its throat slit, hanging in the bathroom. Fear gripped my oesophagus and squeezed. "I'm next!" I thought in terror.

As soon as the woman psychiatrist arrived, I was dragged by the orderlies to her office and stuffed down in a chair opposite her. She looked very worried that day, and for the first time I thought

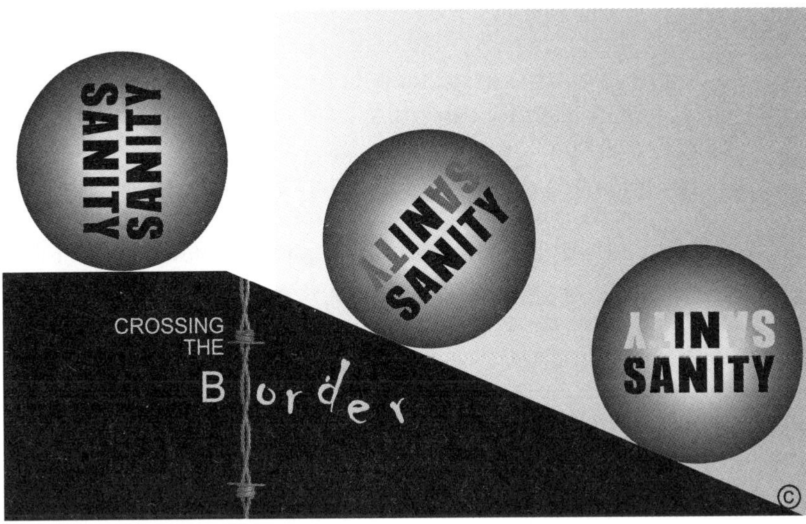
SANITY
SANITY
SANITY
SANITY
IN
SANITY
CROSSING
THE
Border
©

that maybe she had finally seen what was going on. I felt a fleeting glimmer of hope that she might be able to save me.

But hope was crushed instantly by what she said next. "We have decided that there is no option but to give you a course of ECT." She peered at me over her black rims before spelling it out, "… Electro Convulsive Therapy…"

Shock Treatment! Her words stabbed me like a thousand syringes.

Despite my horror at the thought of it, I could have accepted it if it hadn't been for *how* they were proposing to give me the ECT, and more specifically *how many* they had planned. "The programme will start tomorrow. For the next week we will give you *six* treatments. Then you will have a few days' break. Then you will have another *six* treatments. After another few days' break we will administer a final *six* treatments… We have run out of other options."

Six sessions. Six sessions. And Six sessions. *666.* Burnt into my forehead.

> *The Beast forced all men…to have a mark placed on their right hands and on their foreheads. No one could buy and sell unless he had this mark, that is the Beast's name or the number that stands for the name.*

As the sheer horror of it descended upon me, I let out an almighty scream and leapt out of my seat. How I managed it I don't know, but I ran down the corridor, out the front entrance, and down the driveway of the hospital. I had only been able to shuffle for the past few weeks but now pure adrenaline took over. My technicolour dream-coat streamed out behind me in the wind and in one hand I waved my pocket Bible in the air. At the end of the driveway two soldiers jumped out of a guardhouse, brandishing R4 assault rifles. "Repent! Repent for the Rainbow Nation!" I screamed in their faces.

ELECTRO
CONVULSIVE
THERAPY

"The technique is essentially that of passing alternating currents through the head... the passage of the current causes an immediate cessation of consciousness and the induction of a convulsive seizure."

Encyclopaedia Britannica

But it was all in vain. The next thing I knew I was on the ground with my pants down and a male orderly on top of me ramming the syringe of venom into my backside.

Acts 23.9

The next day I lay strapped to an operating table inside a light green tiled room. Plastic tubes ran into my arms and a man with a green hood and mask hovered over a flickering computer screen. The woman psychiatrist was there too, all in black. On a trolley to the right was a small metal device with wires attached to it. It looked rather like a set of headphones, but it was square and shiny. The steel doors behind the psychiatrist shut, and above the door a green light went off, and a red light came on.

I told the psychiatrist to look in my pocket, as there was a note in there for her. I had written it some time the day before. Acts 23:9:

> *We cannot find a thing wrong with this man! Perhaps a spirit or an angel really did speak to him.*

The last thing I remembered was the psychiatrist's eyes. They definitely harboured a touch of sadness.

A Stupid Rifleman

The next thing I was aware of was two excruciating headaches, one pounding on either side of my head. I had a strange taste in my mouth and there was a loud buzzing noise. It took several minutes for the buzzing to organise itself into words and only then did I realise that people were talking. I opened my eyes and there, looking down at me, were the soldiers from Ward 24. The Ping-Ponger, the artist and some of the Shufflers. All present. The nurses were there too, and even one of the male orderlies. "What was it like?" somebody asked, excitedly. I didn't reply for a while. Then: "It was shocking!" and nervous titters of laughter broke out.

The next two weeks are the most vague. ECT is known to lead to severe temporary amnesia. I have vague recollections of excruciating headaches. I remember wandering around not having a clue who I was or where I was. I had lost my mind. Literally.

At some point during those two weeks they convened a military court and I remember sitting outside waiting my turn. I was ushered into a long narrow room and seated on a chair in the middle of the floor. At the head of the room was a raised platform, and on it a row of desks. Behind the desks sat ten people. I remember some of them – the professor, the woman psychiatrist and the day officer. There was also a Colonel.

The psychiatrist sat in the middle and vigorously cleared her throat before addressing me. She had only one sentence for me and it was a question.
"Rifleman, are you a prophet?"
Her words echoed around the silent room and ten pairs of eyes leered down at me, waiting for the profound verdict. A fan hummed in a corner and somewhere in the distance a dove cooed. An incredibly long moment before I replied.
"I don't know". That was the truest answer I could give at that stage. I wasn't sure of anything anymore.

After the sixth session of shock treatment they stopped. Somehow the sixth one had managed to chase Satan away. In a matter of days all spiritual activity evaporated from my world, and I started seeing the same things that everybody else was seeing. I felt like I had landed after a very long and treacherous voyage.

A few days later I got the news about the verdict of the military hearing. Discharged from all further military duty, I would be going home in a matter of days. I guess I should have been happy about it, but I wasn't. Numbness had come over me.

On the day before I left, a military psychologist drove me to another cluster of buildings about three kilometres away. He led me into a room and sat me down on a chair at which a cameraman pointed a large video camera. The interview commenced; he asked me if I realised that smoking dagga had caused my whole experience. “Yes, I’ve realised that,” I said, “and what a stupid rifleman I’ve been”. The cameraman captured it all on film and gave the psychologist a little thumbs up when we left.

The next day I was walking out of the ward in civilian clothes, clutching a large bottle of pills that the doctor had said I must take whenever I didn’t feel well. They warned my parents that in all likelihood I would never be able to hold down a job. The stress would just prove too much, they said. It would be best, they warned my parents, if they didn’t get their hopes up; and they should bank on supporting me for a long, long time.

part II

WHY

Up to now, most scientists have been too occupied with the development of new theories that describe what the universe is, to ask the question why… If we find the answer to that… we would know the mind of God.

A Brief History of Time – Stephen Hawking

A Stranger

No matter what I do, I can't get away from him. I've been running most of the afternoon and I'm absolutely exhausted. I duck into suburban avenues, then into corridors from my old high school, emerging onto golden sun-bleached beaches. But he is always there, a dark, shadowy creature careening across the landscape. In his outstretched hand he carries the branch, a mighty staff of wood with a huge fork at the top. I don't know who he is, nor why he is chasing me, but I know instinctively that I've got to run.

He's getting closer, I can hear his breath now – short rasps of it over the thunder of my feet. I duck behind a hedge and feel the leaves brushing my shoulder. The familiar face of an old friend appears before me, urging me on: "Go Chris…Go!"

I hear the hedge part as he explodes through in pursuit. He's going to catch me any minute now. I can smell his sweat.

The friend yells: "Chris!…Chris!…"

"Chris! Wake up! Chris!" Kate tugs at my shoulder and slowly her worried face comes into focus in the dim light of the bedroom. "You were having nightmares again. Wake up!"

The sheets are sodden with sweat and the blanket lies tangled at my feet.

"Was it that man again… the one with the forked branch?"
"The same…"
"I was so worried about you, you were twitching and moaning." She clutches my arm, "What are we going to do about these nightmares? We can't go on like this".

I lie in silence, not answering her question. What more *can* I do? I've been to the doctor, I'm taking the pills… I'll just have to wait it out… There isn't really any other option.

After about ten minutes, I hear Kate's deep breathing. The red digits of the bedside clock say 2:19am. I wait for sleep to return, but it doesn't come. The same old questions are bouncing around my mind. Who is this persistent character who visits my dreams every other night? What does he want with me? Where does he come from? Why is he always holding that stick? I realise with irritation that I am now wide awake. No chance of sleep after this. Taking care not to make a sound, I get up and pad out of the bedroom.

Y2K

The passage is dimly lit by the light of the single lamp left on in the lounge. I silently thank the ever-practical Kate, who likes to leave at least one light on so we can see our way in the night if necessary. I walk quietly towards the kitchen, my toes sinking luxuriously into the quality woollen carpet. As I pass through the dining-room, running my fingers along the smooth, polished surface of the imposing table, I catch sight of my reflection; a dim silhouette in the huge mirror overhanging the stylish sideboard. "Hmm, need a haircut," I think, ruffling my fringe, and make a mental note to get my personal assistant to book me one in the morning.

In the kitchen, I click on the overhead lights, then dim them a little. The light shines out onto the shiny, curvaceous bonnet of my gun-metal grey Cabriolet, parked outside in the driveway. "Thank God we can afford to live in such a civilised complex with excellent security," I think to myself yet again, "where you don't have to worry about barricading your vehicles for the night".

Kate has left the kitchen sparkling clean before going to bed. I fill the kettle, switch it on, and, reaching into the orderly cupboard for a tea cup and saucer, make myself the perfect cuppa. Taking it through to my study, I settle down at my spacious work desk. I open the broad, wood framed window, to let in the fresh night air. From the dark valley below comes the smell of foliage, moss and wood – fragrant and wild. I sip the tea, taking in the comfortable surroundings. "Not bad," I whisper to myself, but I am not entirely convinced. "Not bad, surely, for a guy who was a certified fruitcake at one stage? I should be happy. And maybe I would be if it weren't for these damned nightmares..."

I *should* be happy! In fact, before the nightmares started, the past fifteen years had been remarkably good considering where I was in 1984.

Sure, following my discharge from hospital I went through a few months of quite serious depression. But within a year I'd enrolled at Pietermaritzburg University and in no time at all the wine, women and song were all flowing once again.

I excelled at university but left campus to get involved in the business world and finished my degree by correspondence. By 21, I owned my own little clothing shop. I sold tie-died T shirts, ethnic pants, brightly coloured beadwork, leather sandals – a welcome relief after the monotones of the SADF. I sold the shop for a profit before entering the field of financial brokering. I did well there too – collecting money, collecting experience and, in my free time, collecting girlfriends.

There were the usual ups and downs. I got caught badly on Black Monday in the stock market crash of '87 and took a year off to recover, hitch-hiking around Europe, Turkey and Israel. Then there was the failed business venture in London. And the unwanted return to South Africa.

"It hasn't always been easy," I surmise, gazing absentmindedly at the lineup of fine Japanese lacquered bowls, in inky black and terracotta, on the window sill, "but right now, as we approach the turn of the millennium, my life's really not in bad shape at all. If it weren't for these damned nightmares…" After all, my latest business venture, an investment brokerage, has really taken off, and I'm flush with cash. I personally look after 50 million Rands worth of my clients' funds, these clients comprising the wealthiest and most astute individuals in the region. They hold me in the highest esteem, respecting my broad-based knowledge of investment markets and my integrity and reliability.

And with the financial success have come the usual spoils – the tastefully decorated five bedroomed home, the Cabrio, and an entertainment budget that would probably comfortably support a dozen poor South African families. There has been no shortage of gorgeous woman either. I fondly recall a long stream of them over the past fifteen years, and the latest, Kate, is a real stunner, and intelligent and sweet too! I'm still young, and definitely Upwardly Mobile. I have youth, health, wealth, education and freedom. Could you get any closer to the American/South African dream?

"Hmm," I say quietly, addressing myself to an imaginary lineup of the psychiatrists, psychologists and army doctors from Ward 24, "I guess I've finally disproved all of *your* dire predictions as to my guaranteed future as a basket case!" I feel momentarily triumphant at my worldly achievements. But then I think of the strange character pursuing me in the dream, and my heart sinks.

He'd been visiting me for about a month, and now the visits had started impacting on my daylight hours too. At first it was just a vague niggle, one that would crop up every week or so. But soon I found myself questioning the meaning of my whole existence. Despite my achievements, my confidence and my worldly possessions, something was missing.

My initial strategy to outwit the lurking feeling of meaninglessness and despondency was to throw myself ever more ferociously into my daily routine of wealth accumulation and protection. On the rare occasion that hadn't worked, I found that a night out with a good bottle of whisky would wash away the doubts.

But when I closed my eyes and tried to rest at night, the shadowy creature with the forked branch was back. On countless occasions I'd awaken around 2am and toss and turn until daylight. Then I'd be unable to drag myself out of bed. It had got to the stage where, on really bad days, I couldn't get out of bed at all, but would lie with the duvet pulled over my head, shutting out the noisy world for as long as I could, and feeling numb. When I did make it to work, I was drained, painfully aware that a growing despondency was steadily sapping my energy. I felt like a fraud, acting the part of the confident, upbeat businessman; dispensing financial wisdom, giving people answers and advice, while privately feeling miserable, lost and empty.

Kate even thought I might have contracted some type of virus (yuppie flu perhaps), and on her insistence I dragged myself off to see my local GP. Half an hour later, I'd left the doctor's rooms with a prescription for six months' worth of Prozac (the first psychiatric pills for over a decade), and the diagnosis of "serious depression" bouncing around in my mind.

Clues

Suddenly the "miraculous recovery" of the past fifteen years no longer looked so good. My business was still booming (probably only because I had such excellent staff), but I could no longer claim to be in good health. Increasingly, I struggled to make conversation with people. I felt disconnected when in crowds, and fearful when put under pressure. The endless invitations to industry functions, the well-meaning attempts to book me for public speaking engagement, would throw me into a state of panic; my secretary, poor woman, was becoming skilled at lying and covering up for me, although I hadn't told her how bad things really were. Kate too was starting to be alarmed at my volatile moods and desire to avoid social contact. It really seemed that I could no longer afford to ignore the demon that had hijacked my night-time mind.

Kate bought me a whole pile of self-help books from the library. On the pretext of a bad dose of flu', I took a week's sick leave. I banned my staff from dropping in or phoning, and committed myself seriously to the project of scouring the pages of the books to see if I could shed any light on my predicament. Within a few days I came across a sentence that shook me awake:

> *The lesson is this: Your life tells you your path if you stop to look at the clues it has been throwing at you all of this time.*[3]

I wrote down the sentence and showed it to Kate. "An interesting quotation", she said. "So, what clues have you found?" Kate didn't like unsolved problems hanging around!
"None yet."
"Maybe there are some clues in your dream?" She looked hopeful.
"Maybe…"
I had read and re-read the quotation "*...stop to look at the clues...stop to look at the clues...*" It sounded so simple – but it wasn't. For the first time I realised that I'd been so immersed in the pursuit of wealth these past few years, that I hadn't taken stock of where I was coming from or where I was going for a long, long time.

I had two chairs in my study: one "swivel chair" in front of the computer monitor, and one armchair in the corner by the bookcase. I had always spent most of my time in the swivel chair, tapping figures and letters into my hard drive. But that spring of 1999, faced with the task of finding clues, I resolved to spend more time in the armchair, just sitting and thinking about things. It was essential for my "Stopping and Looking" strategy, the strategy that I was entrusting to outsmart the "serious depression" diagnosis.

It was on this night, then, when my latest nightmare kept me from sleep, and I had drained the last dregs of my cup of tea, that I got up from my desk and settled myself in my armchair,

---

[3] Geri Larkin

to think. And it was there, a short while later, that I made the first connection.

Inexplicably at the time, my mind returned to my experience in Ward 24, fifteen years earlier. I recalled the Shufflers, and the artist, and Satan's horrific Sergeant. It all seemed so far away now. Like a different era, a different time zone, a different person… I recalled the little black cat that had been sacrificed… I recalled the smug professor at the other end of the hospital and the twig of driftwood on his table… the twig of driftwood on his table… the twig of driftwood on his table. *THAT WAS IT*! The twig was Y shaped, the same as the one that the man in the nightmare carried. That was the clue!

Explanations

For fifteen years I had tried my best to forget about Ward 24. Everyone had encouraged me to do this. After all, undergoing a psychotic breakdown is not considered an achievement but rather something to be locked up in the closet, with the rest of the family secrets!

Not many people in my current life knew about my army experiences. I'd told Kate a little, but definitely not the full story. But now, as I told her the next morning about my discovery of the Y shaped twig clue, she was adamant, "Well, the two branches have definitely got something to do with each other. Of course they have! You'd have to be blind not to see that…"

So, like it or not I was forced to face 1984 again. There were still plenty of unanswered questions surrounding my whole excursion into insanity but the biggest question was "*Why*?"

Why had those incredible things happened to me in 1984? Prior to my conscription I had led a relatively normal life and knew very little about psychosis or Schizophrenia. True, on one occasion I'd been sent by my high school to see a psychologist. But that was because I had scored astronomically high results on a routine IQ test and the school had been concerned about my "lack of academic ambition".

Back in the aftermath of Ward 24, there had been no shortage of official explanations for my nervous breakdown. The drug theory was the one favoured by the SADF and was also supported by a psychiatrist in private practice in Durban who had taken over the management of my medication. They postulated that the *dagga* had triggered a chemical imbalance in my brain. I wasn't the first, they had assured me, who had started out on a bad trip and ended up in a psychiatric ward. Some of us are genetically pre-disposed to such things, they had explained, and more often than not, the more intelligent ones. After all, goes the argument, there has always been a mysteriously close link between genius and psychosis. (In the early 1990s, after passing the entry test, I was admitted to the international High IQ society, MENSA, which seemed to confirm both the school tests and some of the thinking of the psychiatrists.)

This "drug theory" particularly suited the military, as it absolved them of any guilt. Nevertheless, my full army pay arrived mysteriously in my bank account for over a year after I had been discharged. I accepted the money, but always with the niggling suspicion that it was partly a guilt payment!

The second possible theory about "*why* it had happened" concerned my military duty in Angola: post-traumatic stress disorder. This phenomenon had first been observed in the Vietnam war when young soldiers suddenly developed psychotic symptoms about six months after experiencing combat. This timeframe would have been about right for me. Six months prior to my hospitalisation, I had been involved in a series of skirmishes in southern Angola. I was only 19 years old at the time, a mere teenager, and although I was never physically injured, the stress and fear must surely have had an influence. (About three months after being discharged from the army, I received a letter to attend a military parade at Natal Command where I was to be awarded a *Pro Patria* medal for border service for my country. I never attended.)

Another possible explanation for "*why* it had happened" – my family background. Dad: a brilliant Chemical Engineer with a PhD *cum laude* to prove it; a rigid scientific man against whom I rebelled violently in my youth. By the time I got to my teens, there was so much hatred between us that when he went away on business trips, I used to wish he wouldn't come back. I lost all interest in school life and opted, instead, to spend all my time with a group of dropouts who smoked grass and listened to reggae. We were anti-school, anti-government and anti-establishment. I was the eternal black sheep of the family at that time, and experienced very little love in my high school days.

It wasn't just me that my father clashed with – he clashed with my mother too, from ever since I could remember. Mom: the artist. Sociable, expressive, sensual, flamboyant; a person whose creative, intuitive style of thinking didn't always fit in with my father's structured scheme of things. My father had a foul temper in those days and his shouting and verbal abuse were everyday trademarks of our home.

I think my father had hoped the army would straighten me out. "It's high time somebody knocked some sense into him," he'd say. But prior to my hospitalisation, the army hadn't changed me at all, certainly not on the outside, and my father and I had been involved in some almighty clashes in the weeks prior to that time.

I have no doubt that all of these theories about "*why* it had happened" had some truth in them. But now, as I looked back with a fresh perspective, I suspected that there had to be some deeper *reason* – something that could tell me more about my current life and where I was going. Something more than just another unfortunate chemical and situational occurrence. Something that could help explain why now, fifteen years later, by night a sinister man with a forked branch chased me around in my dreams!

And so began my search for the real "*why* it had happened".

The Question

In retrospect the search had actually begun shortly after my release from hospital, although at the time I was unaware what it was I was searching for. In 1985, when I first enrolled at Pietermaritzburg University, it was to study philosophy, religious studies and psychology. Not commerce – which was the field in which I eventually graduated.

One thing that I'd learnt from my hospital experience was that you could not take anything for granted; one day the world can seem normal and the next the whole system can fall apart. I therefore began to question *everything* – thoroughly testing the ground around me before taking a step. Philosophy seemed to be the right medium through which to conduct this questioning and I excelled in my studies. But I can see now that I was not ready at that stage to learn the wisdom of my experiences. Before I knew it I was entangled in a bittersweet romance and left university for more lucrative pursuits, where the prospect of sexy women, fast cars and a flashy lifestyle beckoned.

The short spell of formal philosophic discipline was never totally wasted though. The times I sat in my armchair in the study pondering "*why* it had happened", I could see the merits of the analytic method. With the day at the office behind me, and my door firmly closed on the outside world, I began rigorously re-examining possible reasons for my experiences.

Philosophy does many things but perhaps the most important thing it does is "examine its own grounds". Where other branches of knowledge attempt to answer various questions, philosophy takes a step backwards and looks at the question itself. "Finding the right questions is more important than the right answers", my old philosophy professor used to say.

The question I was looking at was, "*Why?*". An extremely interesting question, it stands alone in a unique category, apart from the wheres?, whens?, whos?, whats?, whiches? and hows? of the world. These questions merely provide information on the co-ordinates of an entity or event in space and time. They do not give any real meaning about the thing itself. "*Why?*", on the other hand, digs deeper. "*Why?*" seeks reasons and reasons are more meaningful than co-ordinates.

A good way to illustrate the unique nature of "*Why?*" is to apply the full spectrum of questions to evolution (a fitting topic because it surely rates as one of the greatest theories of western science). Evolution explains *when* life began, *which* life began, *where* life began, and even *how* life began. But ask an evolutionist *why* life began and you will be met by a stunned silence.

Evolution is not the only topic that bypasses the "*Why?*" question. Countless issues go begging for reasons. Important issues such as: "Why are we born?"; "Why do we die?"; "Why do we fight and wage wars against one another?"

Society does not always encourage "*Why?*"questions. And not surprisingly. If the employees on a conveyor belt in a great factory were suddenly to take a little time out to think about why they were doing what they were doing, the factory would come to a standstill. If the soldier stopped in his tracks and asked why he was about to murder the stranger in his sights, wars would fall apart. The system would land up in a state of mayhem. And so, in order to keep the cogs of civilisation turning, the vast majority

THE Y FACTOR

THE Y FACTORY

THE Y FACTORY

THE Y FACTORY

THE FACTORY©

THE CONVERSION PROCESS

of us stumble through our lives without knowing why we do the things we do.

But we didn't start out not knowing. No sooner does a child start talking, than the why questions start popping out – "Why?" "Why?" "Why?" "Why, Mom, why?". Infuriating to our conditioned adult minds – and not least because a long trail of whys invariably leads back to a fundamental "*Why?*" to which we ourselves do not have the answer.

Perhaps a good way to explain the unique nature of "*Why?*" is to borrow a definition I once came across during my first year of university economics. The definition had to do with the two goals of any enterprise: efficiency and effectiveness. Efficiency is *doing things right*, while effectiveness is about *doing the right things.*

Efficiency is all about "know-how", who is to do what, where, when and especially how. The whos, whats, wheres and whens are merely co-efficients – factors of production in the great efficient factory of life. The theory of evolution displays this really well. Isn't evolution merely the survival of the most efficient?

Doing the right things is a little more complicated. To find out what is right as opposed to what is wrong we need to ask ourselves: "Why are we doing what we are doing?" The question "*Why?*" will ultimately be answered with a "because". Important, because very often the clues to meaning are contained in the words themselves. Take the word "because". When we are answered with a "be*cause*", we then have the *cause* of our actions. The cause naturally leads to the effect (cause and effect) and once we approach the effect from the cause, we can know effectiveness. So effectiveness is "know-why", as opposed to "know-how". Our modern technological world seems obsessed with "know-how" (usually at the expense of know-why). Hitler's Nazis were efficient, but were they doing the right things?

I suppose it was understandable that I should become obsessed with the question "*Why?*" after my hospitalisation. After all, what is insanity, other than irrational behaviour resulting from the loss of your faculties of reason? That's the link – *reason*. Asking "*Why?*" leads to reasons and reasons lead to Reason. When someone has experienced a total loss of reason, it's not surprising that, at some stage, he would embark on an extensive search for reasons. It seemed the sane thing to do.

The search for reason is not new. Ever since the days of Socrates the main foundation of western philosophy has been reason. The Enlightenment, that golden period of western civilisation when we emerged from the long and depraved centuries of the Dark Ages, is also known as the Age of Reason. And it was the Rationalists (the school of scientists and philosophers who expounded the virtues of reason), who shed light on the stifling and corrupt dogma of the previous era.

Therefore, as I set out on my journey, searching for meaning in my floundering mid-life, I armed myself with the question "*Why?*". For "*Why?*" would lead to reason and reason would lead to meaning and meaning would lead me to my personal Enlightenment (or so I hoped).

A Crooked Letter

It was at about this time that I made the second important connection in my philosophising. One night after I'd been awakened by yet another nightmare Kate asked, "Did he have the Y stick again?"

"He did… the Y stick, the bloody Y stick…"

But that night the stick stuck in my mind and I made the groundbreaking connection between Y and "*Why?*"

Had Y not always been the crooked letter? The one that you couldn't make straight?

Acoustic Knots

Most of my philosophising was done in my study in the evenings. Every night after supper I'd retreat there, shutting the door firmly on my daytime reality, and on Kate. Sometimes I'd read, sometimes I'd surf the internet, other times I would just sit in the chair under the bookcase and think. It was a cosy and comfortable room – I'd painted the walls a burnt orange and an African rug warmed the floor. The wide window overlooked the valley of a nature reserve and it was still and peaceful at night.

It wasn't long before my evening investigations, which had commenced with the seemingly innocent question "*Why?*", had developed into a fully fledged Quest. During the days I continued plugging away at my financial routines, but it was the nights that I was living for. Despite Kate's protests, I was, I must admit, starting to feel a bit better. That feeling of despondency was lifting, I thought. In time I even began to regard my nocturnal activities as another job. I was moonlighting – a financial advisor by day; an aspiring philosopher by night.

At first I figured that maybe the Y/*why* connection was merely a coincidence. But after a week or two I rationalised that even if it were a coincidence it could still be important to my investigation. In fact, coincidences could be said to have a peculiar relationship with the question "*Why?*" because, by definition, coincidences are events that mysteriously come together *without any apparent reason*. (For, if they did possess reasons and had a "be*cause*", they would no longer be termed coincidences, but merely effects of some explainable cause in the universe.) Coincidences were, it seemed to my fascinated mind, a category of events that managed to evade the question "*Why?*"

I began to recall how the whole Ward 24 experience had seemed to start with a series of coincidences. They had become more and more uncanny. Surely they possessed in their depths some greater underlying reason? Or was I just reading too much into the situation? Should we really dismiss coincidences – seemingly filled with personal meaning and import – as merely random, not to be taken seriously? For that would be the western, scientific understanding. The clever evolutionist, I am sure, could even attribute the whole of creation to coincidence; a random coming together of the right chemicals, at the right time, in the right way, but with no deeper reasons. (How fortunate though, for all of us sitting here on planet earth today, that such a "coincidence" occurred!)

Some people pass through their lives totally oblivious to coincidences. A connoisseur, on the other hand, can probably find at least one good one per week. So, there seem to be two schools of thought about coincidences: the first maintains that their occurrence is random and arbitrary, not to be remarked or examined more closely for deeper meaning; the second believes their occurrence is significant, not random or arbitrary at all, but a potential source of wisdom and personal meaning.

What was drawing me to the second school of thought was that the coincidences in my life did not end after my release from Ward 24. Certainly there have been long spells of drought when I have been so immersed in the everyday pursuit of money that nothing deeper than Rands or cents has registered on my personal radar screen. But there had been other patches in between when the occurrence rate of coincidences had inexplicably soared and yanked me out of my everyday patterns, giving me a heightened sense of what was going on around me in the greater world. Some of the coincidences had even been linked to my Ward 24 experiences.

In one of them, I was driving down the road several years after 1984, thinking about the Angolan reconnaissance operation, when the name of the operation, which had long since eluded me, suddenly popped into my mind: Operation Omega. At that time, I was driving an Alpha Romeo.

Another time, I'd been thinking about the shock treatment I had received, thankful that they had only given me the first set of six and not the following two sets of six. I had only received one third of the original plan. Which left two thirds. I was on my way to an accountancy exam at the time and my mind was in mathematical mode. The 2/3 fraction tossed around in my mind for a while and then suddenly converted itself to decimal places which flashed out in front of me as if on a giant screen: 0,666 666 666 recurring... Recurring...

But it was my discovery of a special type of coincidence that really accelerated my Quest. This type of coincidence had been central to my own psychosis: the Code; the pun. Eloquently described as "*an acoustic knot, which ties two different meanings together*",[4] the pun unites two formerly unrelated things for no apparent reason. Now this is also exactly what a coincidence does.

Once again, I called upon my sacred question... "*Why?*" Why do some words with different meanings coincide in the same sound? Is there a deeper (hidden) reason? Was there perhaps something more than psychosis in the Code that I had identified in hospital? Was there a link between my recurring nightmare and the Code? Was there some unfinished business?

Arbitrary Signs

By now it was clear that my philosophical investigations were going to require some input from other philosophers, and I hauled out my old university books. I had allocated them a special place on my bookshelf all those years ago, and there they had remained.

My days in the office were getting shorter and my nights in the study longer, but my business had a surprising supply of momentum and managed to keep going under its own steam. Kate, however, was not so unproblematic! She'd started complaining that I was "spending too much time locked up in that room on your own".

---

[4] **Encyclopaedia Britannica**

I'd met Kate in an inebriated state, at a bar a year previously. Sometimes I wondered if this relationship was going anywhere in the longer term – we seemed so different, and the more so since I'd become less interested in pursuing her, and more absorbed in pursuing my Quest. She was quite a catch, though, and I was aware that her long hair flowing out next to me in the Cabrio as we jetted down the highway made an impressive picture. I wasn't yet ready to make any decisions about my future with Kate.

From time to time she'd knock on the study door to offer me tea. When the door opened she'd scan the piles of books and papers with keen suspicion. Her original enthusiasm for this "finding clues" project seemed to be wearing thin, to be replaced by a mixture of cynicism and hurt. "I don't understand why you need to spend so many hours in here on your own," she said, petulantly, "I don't think it's healthy!"
"*I'm* not healthy, Kate! I'm having nightmares. I'm on pills again. I feel down. That's precisely why I need to spend time in here thinking!" I said, my explanation a triumph of logic over whingeing.

Undeterred, I forged onwards with my Quest. What made puns particularly useful was that, of all the types of coincidences, puns are the easiest to work with. Most coincidences involve a timing element that mysteriously brings together different events, but puns have a timeless character that makes them more susceptible to analysis. If I could somehow prove that puns possessed deeper reasons, I'd be in a good position to prove that other coincidences contained deeper reasons too. And maybe I'd fathom the night-time visitor waving the forked branch.

In order to determine whether there are any deeper reasons for two words sharing the same sound, I figured that it would be necessary to find the reasons for the independent words themselves. This leads into the very complicated field of linguistics

– a branch of philosophy with which philosophers have become increasingly preoccupied. One of the most famous philosophers of the 20th century, Ludwig Wittgenstein, even suggested, “The sole remaining task for philosophy is the analysis of language”.

In everyday life, we are inclined to take language for granted. Yet language is humankind’s greatest achievement. Undoubtedly, language is the single most important feature that distinguishes us from the apes. A good exercise to demonstrate just how much we take language for granted is to take a word (any word) and repeat it aloud, over and over again, concentrating on how the word sounds. One of my favourite words for this exercise is “clumsy”, but you can take your pick. Any word will do. Repeat it enough times, and eventually the word will start to sound quite bizarre and you will see it in a totally new light.

(A little word of warning here: do this exercise in private. The night I tried it, I was sitting in the lounge – to disprove Kate’s theory that I was “always locked away in the study”. When she walked into the room, I can promise you that the look on her face was not encouraging.)

Language is a medium. Words serve as the link between the world and our minds. Two very important components inhabit this equation – the word (the sign) and the "thing" it refers to (the referent). Usually words have one-on-one relationships with their referents but in the case of a pun, there are two (or sometimes more) referents.

Take the word “branch”. According to the **Collins English Dictionary**, there are two distinct meanings for branch. Firstly it is “*a secondary woody stem extending from the trunk... of a tree*”. Secondly, it is “*a sub-division or subsidiary section of something larger or more complex... e.g. branch of philosophy*”. So the one meaning equates to “twig” and the other meaning equates to “section”. Diagrammatically it could be represented like this:

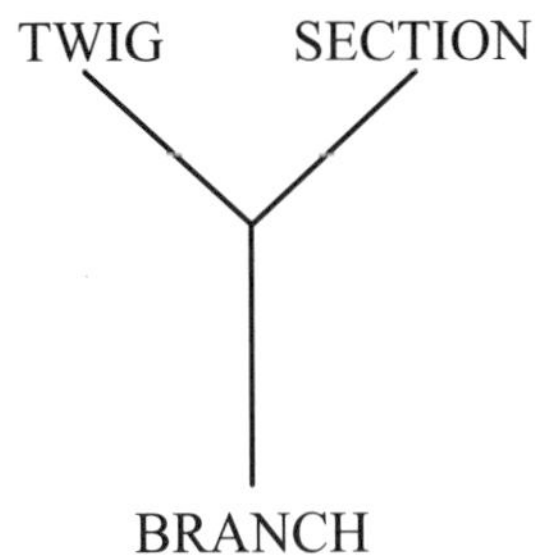

The important question relating to my Quest was this: “*Why* do these two referents share one sign?” In order to find this out, we need to examine very closely the relation between a sign and its referent. Why were the letters B R A N C H chosen to represent the twig of a tree? Is there something about the qualities of the letters that corresponds with the qualities of a twig? After all, the first branch didn't just fall out of the sky with “branch” written on it. And why is a twig called a “twig”?

Maybe “branch” is not such a clear example. But take the words:

SI
FRIC
RABI
MERIC

Do you recognise them? Maybe if I add the following two it will become clearer:

USTRALI
NTARCTIC

Getting it yet? These words are the names for the continents minus the letter A: Asia, Africa, Arabia, America, Australia and Antarctica. The important question is "*Why?*" Why do all the continent's names start with an A and end in an A? Is it merely arbitrary coincidence? Or is there some deeper reason?

It took me several nights of moonlight research and a trip to the university library to unravel some answers. But the orthodox answer was not particularly helpful to my cause. According to the most respected modern linguists, *there is definitely no deeper reason*. The "founder" of linguistics, Ferdinand de Saussure, focused right at the very start on the relationship between sign and referent. He realised that this was the crux of the whole theory of linguistics. In his opinion, the relationship between sign and referent was *arbitrary*. Totally random. Any word could have been used for any thing, and the word/world pattern is, ultimately, entirely haphazard. This was an alarming conclusion for me; with puns I had evidently arrived at the same dead-end I'd arrived at with coincidences – meaningless randomness.

There was a significant body of highly logical and acclaimed theory to try to get around, and I thought for a while that my Quest was doomed to an early death. Maybe my whole Ward 24 experience was not a meaningful clue to my life's path after all, but rather a random and arbitrary twist of events that might have happened to anybody. Maybe it was just a case, fifteen year previously, of being in the wrong place at the wrong time. Certainly that's what seemed to be echoing back at me from the theories of the greatest western philosophers.

Speaking in Tongues

It wasn't always easy pursuing my Quest. I was painfully aware that the evening occupation that I had acquired would not make for good small talk with my fellow financial advisor colleagues. Nor was it something I could chat about with my clients or staff. "Have you had any good coincidences lately?" doesn't fit the lip

SI

FRIC

RABI

MERIC

USTRALI

NTARTIC ©

CONTINENTAL
DRIFT

of an investment broker. "So, what's your opinion on the arbitrary relationship between signs and referents? Hmm?" Or, "Ever thought seriously about '*Why?*'" My clients would jump ship faster than sinking sea captains, and my staff would probably rush to visit psychologists. Hell, even Kate was beginning to eye me warily whenever our conversations looked like they might stray towards the less-than-concrete.

Instead, I made small talk with my clients about the rugby, the cricket and the weather. In their eyes I was surely a "common or garden variety" financial advisor. White male. Medium build. Dark hair. Well groomed. Obviously educated. A regular sort of guy. If only they knew…

I felt more and more like an imposter. There seemed an increasing gulf between the regular, "daytime Chris", who played by the rules of the corporate world, and the "night-time Chris" – toying, under cover of darkness, with obscure theories and bizarre thoughts. To reconcile the contradiction, I convinced myself that I was just playing by the rules of some grand capitalistic etiquette. Wasn't all business like this? What was the function of Public Relations departments in large corporations, other than to present the corporation in its sugar-coated version? After all, not even high court judges were impervious to a witness's "outward disposition". A sharp lawyer will always advise you to get a good suit. Books get judged by their covers every day.

And so, despite my daily masquerade, I proceeded with my nocturnal activities. I decided that if I was going to prove a link between world and word, my first prong of attack should be to follow the evolution of various words back to their roots. For surely, if there were a tangible link, that link had to be found at the word's beginning – at the time when the word was "chosen" to signify some aspect of the world. This search took me into another branch of linguistics – etymology – the study of the evolution of words. ("No, Kate, not e*n*tymology!" I'd pointed out, a bit patronisingly I suppose, to her hopeful comment that "This should be more interesting than fiddling around with boring *words* all the time". She'd looked wounded.)

I started collecting dictionaries, the standard type and those specialising in word histories. Dictionaries, I have found, are one of the most valuable tools in quests of a philosophic nature. All quests are ultimately a search for meaning, and dictionaries are the end-of-the-line authorities when it comes to the verbatim aspect of meaning. They are a rich source of clues because, so often, the clue that is overlooked is contained in the word itself. Or to put it another way: the *spell* is in the *spell*ing.

I was to unearth many valuable links in my dictionary wanderings. However, I never found the big breakthrough – the one that would provide irrefutable evidence that the link between words and world was not arbitrary. Once again, I became somewhat discouraged. Perhaps I was wasting my time? Perhaps I should just content myself with my business success and focus my energies on more practical matters? But I had a horrible premonition that if I did, the night-time demon would never leave me. I couldn't face the prospect of his company for the rest of my life.

One evening, exasperated after a week of stressful dealings in my business and a week of dead-ends in my Quest, I was settling myself down with a bottle of Jack Daniels when something on TV caught my eye. An old Western movie. A distinguished looking Apache chief, arguing with a young gun-slinging cowboy, said: "White man speak with forked tongue!" For some reason, the words stuck with me and played themselves over in my mind for the next few days. Of course I knew what the analogy meant – it meant that the white man couldn't be trusted because he said one thing and did another.

It was about a week later, in the small hours of the morning, that the image invaded my dreams. I shot bolt upright, sweating, from a deep sleep.
“What's wrong? Was it the branch man again?” Kate asked, her voice trembling.
“No. The man wasn't there. This time there was a snake... a huge snake… chasing me.”
In the dream it had been a black serpent; out of its mouth had darted a bright red, forked tongue.

The next evening, while sitting in my study collecting myself after the day's masquerade, I made another groundbreaking connection. It struck me that the serpent's tongue was very similar in shape and structure to the diagram I had previously drawn to depict the double meaning of the pun:

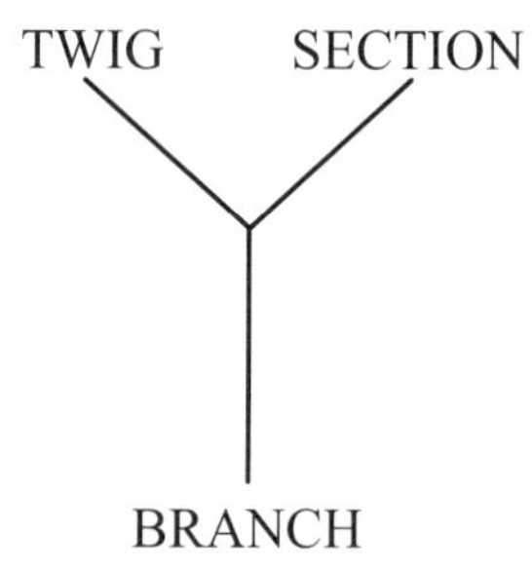

More importantly, both the pun and the forked tongue seemed to result in a split of meanings! There *had* to be a link! Images of snakes filled my mind and before long, the most notorious of them all popped up – the original serpent of biblical myth that had deceived humankind into eating from the Tree of Knowledge of good and evil. Was not the forked tongue the cause of humankind's fall from grace?

The next connection seemed to emerge from somewhere between the image of the snake and the shape of the snake's tongue. I became aware that, just as the snake's tongue was shaped like the letter Y, so too was its body shaped like the letter S. And with that realisation, I stumbled upon another coincidence; that the word "serpent" and the word "snake" both commence with the letter S. What's more, the sound of an S is remarkably similar to the hiss of a snake. Had the first ancient speakers been inspired by a snake when they designed the letter S, or was it just another arbitrary coincidence?

It was a great theory but I needed an acid test. If S did have an enigmatic link to the serpent then surely this link would have surfaced in other languages too? I looked up some translation sites on the internet, and what I found was uncanny. The word snake began with an S in German, French, Spanish, Danish, Dutch, Italian and even Japanese.

Not only did my S discovery indicate some tangible link between letter and world, it also exposed what I believed was a gigantic flaw in the leading linguists' theories. Linguistics entails breaking language down into its constituent parts – into sentences and finally into words. The word, they argue, is the ultimate building block and that is where the understanding should start. And that is where I, too, had launched my previous attack on the arbitrary sign – on the word level. But now I considered the possibility that we had all made a mistake. For words are not, after all, the most fundamental building blocks of language. There is a whole level beneath words, which is the level of *letters*. Just as sentences hold language together and words hold sentences together; *letters hold words together.*

An Egyptian God

Even though Kate wasn't completely sure what I was up to behind my closed doors at night, she did realise that my daytime persona was a mask. She knew it wasn't the real me that sat politely with

A TWIST IN THE TAIL

clients. But she also understood the necessity of the act. She worked in packaging, after all, and what we did was not dissimilar. Just as I dressed up my persona to appeal to my clients, she dressed up her products to appeal to hers. And her department was booming. "It's not just a fad," she said, "packaging is becoming more and more important in our consumer society. It's the wrapper that makes the sale".

And so during the day our wrappers continued making sales. But it was the night-time that was really getting interesting. Spurred on by the discovery of a level below words, I embarked on an exhaustive search into the origins of the alphabet. More books, more encyclopedias and more websites. If there was to be a link between words and the outside world, maybe the link was to be found on the letter level. For days, I scoured for clues and was taken back first to the ancient Greeks, then to the Phoenicians, and then to the Hebrews and Egyptians.

We tend to take the letters we use today for granted, but I learnt in my research that the further back I went and the closer I got to writing's origins, the more sacred the letters became (the word hieroglyphics actually means "sacred writing"). Many Hebrews believe that the original letters were personally handed to us by God himself. To this day, in fact, the Jewish mystic school of the Kabala advocates that each letter of the Hebrew alphabet contains divine secrets and the faithful are encouraged to meditate upon individual Jewish letters. Maybe John the apostle was right, "In the beginning was the word, and the word was God".

Due to the alphabet's antiquity, its exact origin is fiercely contested. Strictly speaking, Egyptian hieroglyphics does not qualify as a contender, as it is a syllabary rather than a phonetic alphabet. Most theories seem to point in the direction of the wandering Hebrews somewhere in the lands of Ancient Canaan.

One town kept cropping up in my research. I have no doubt that, while this town may not have given birth to the phonetic alphabet, it was surely instrumental in its early development. The town still exists today as the modern port of Jubayi on the Lebanese coast, but in ancient times it was an important Phoenician port known as Byblos.

And so I ventured into ancient Byblos, eager to find my link between word and world, eager to disprove the arbitrary relationship between puns and coincidences, and eager to find out why I had gone psychotic in 1984. I was particularly on the lookout for the origins of individual letters such as Y, as this letter seemed to be playing a larger and larger role in my life.

After paging through what now seems like hundreds of musty old tomes, it was in Byblos that I first came upon the spoor. I had been scanning table upon table of letters, and photographs and diagrams of ancient slabs of inscribed rock. (Most of the inscriptions looked more like undecipherable squiggles and lines than these letters that you are now reading.)

Eventually I came across a stela that had been dug up in Byblos, with 36 "letters" engraved upon it in neat rows. Amongst those letters, a full five were startlingly similar to the cross on which Jesus would be crucified some 600 years later. More importantly, though, the symbol on the top right hand corner looked just like a Y. Not only did it look like a Y, but the way it was drawn made it distinctly resemble the branch of a tree.

Encouraged by my finding, I undertook some further investigation into the ancient port of Byblos, on whose shores had landed many visitors from the land of Egypt. Most of these visitors were not particularly notable, but there was one who stands out head and shoulders above the rest, and not least because of the manner in which he arrived in the ancient port – he washed up on the shores of Byblos in his own coffin. This distinguished visitor was none other than the great Egyptian deity, Osiris.

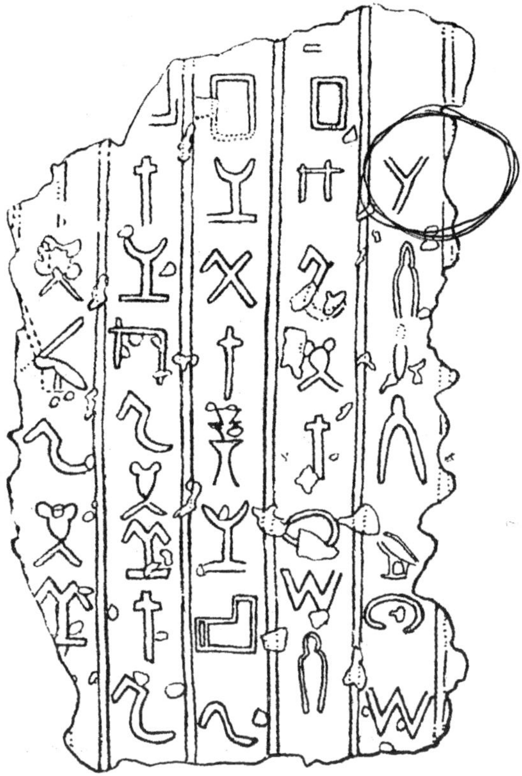

10.4*a*. Stone inscription from Byblos (stele g).

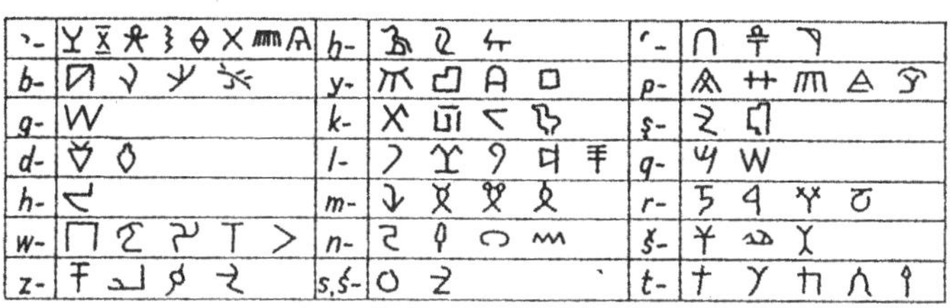

10.4*b*. The pseudo-hieroglyphic syllabary of Byblos according to Dhorme.

Photocopy of stela (top) on page 122 of David Deringer's **The Alphabet: A Key to the History of Mankind** (1948), showing a branch-like Y.

Osiris. One of the mightiest gods of ancient Egypt. God of the Underworld, he was believed to inhabit two worlds simultaneously: the everyday world; and the Other world, the one across the Great Divide, on the other side of death. Statues and pictures always depict Osiris holding two different instruments across his chest, one in each hand. The instruments represent his dual roles. For, while other Egyptian Gods reigned in either one or the other world, Osiris alone possessed the unique quality that allowed him to serve as a divine medium between both.

How Osiris acquired this unique quality is where Byblos comes into the story. Before reaching the Other world, Osiris was murdered by his betraying god-brother, Seth, and cut up into little pieces that were placed inside a coffin. The coffin was cast adrift onto the waters of the Nile, and after several weeks at sea, finally washed up on the shores of Byblos. No sooner had the coffin come to rest, so the legend goes, than a giant, magical tree sprouted forth beneath the coffin and lifted it out of the salty waters into the safety of an enormous forked branch. Once out of the water, Osiris reincarnated in the spirit world and reclaimed his godly status. It was the forked branch of the magical tree that ultimately saved Osiris. And the King of Byblos was so pleased that he commissioned the tree to be replanted in his palace garden where its forked branches could be seen by all who entered the kingdom.

The ancient inhabitants of Byblos must surely have known of this myth. Locals would have revered such a divine visit. And the mystical tree with its magical branches must have been a symbol of great significance. Was this image of the mystical tree in the mind of the scribe who carved the letter Y onto the great stela? Could this stela be my personal Rosetta Stone, the one that would finally provide me with the non-arbitrary link between letter and world? Could this letter be the one constant to which I could anchor my whole theory of meaning in this detached and shifting sea of randomness?

YHWH

One night, when Kate sleepily asked why I was coming to bed so late and I told her that I had been researching Egyptian gods, she snapped on the light and sat up, blinking. I had to stop myself from laughing; she looked quite comical with her wildly rumpled hair, and pursed lips.

"You haven't been forgetting to take your pills have you?" Her concern was genuine. "You know Chris, you really are taking this thing a bit too far. Imagine what your clients would think if they knew what you did at night? This is getting… *weird*. And my mom agrees with me! Why can't you just be normal and happy with what you've got in life?"

Kate was right. Maybe these theories were bordering on the irrational. I mean, how in the world could an ancient Egyptian god be muddled up with my recurring nightmares? As alluring as the ancient ports of Phoenicia were, it was in a sober mood that I accepted that they were not going to give me the hard and credible evidence to overthrow the Random School of Philosophy! I therefore curtailed my adventures into Phoenicia. "Maybe," I pondered the next evening in my study, "in Byblos I have been *barking up the wrong tree*".

But I didn't give up the search altogether. Within a week I was back on the trail and this time I turned my attention to the Old Testament lands, where consensus had placed the birth of the alphabet. I scrutinised the Hebrew alphabet for clues, specifically the Hebrew letter "Yod", from which the letter Y is said to have originated. Yod was the tenth letter and in the ancient doctrines of the Kabala, its numerical value (for mystical purposes) was also ten. An auspicious letter, there were rumours that it was the first letter to be created. It was certainly the smallest Hebrew letter. But I could not find any other clues.

Maybe the Hebrews were leading me up the garden path too? Kate would certainly have said so. I was about to pack them in, when I came across the four letters YHWH. This "word" is probably the most sacred combination of letters in Hebrew and is known as the Tetragamaton. We know the word today as Yahweh (YaHWeH). According to Jewish tradition, this is the personal name of God as revealed to Moses. So revered is this name that, even in our times, many Jews believe that it is too holy for utterance.

How did it suddenly come to me that if you reversed the letters, you would get HWHY? From there it was simply a matter of deleting the first H, and you would be left with the central word of my entire Quest – "*Why?*" Was this yet another "arbitrary" coincidence or was it a meaningful clue?

Whatever it was, it rekindled my faltering Quest. It reminded me that I still did not know exactly *why* 1984 had happened. And I took a vow, there and then: "I will never rest until the day I find a meaningful reason for my experiences".

Ultimately the true value of the Tetragamaton was to lie not in its question "*Why?*", but in another anomaly. The word lacked vowels. This was not an earth-shattering finding, but it warranted further research. I soon found that the original Hebrew alphabet comprised 22 letters and did not contain any vowels. It was only the Greeks, later on, who invented the vowels we use today.

This seemed bizarre, as speech becomes impossible without vowels. How did the ancient Hebrews manage to speak? I learnt that the Hebrews *did* use vowels in their speech; they simply omitted vowels in the written word. Why was this so?

What differentiates vowels from consonants is that vowels are the sounding aloud of unimpeded breath, whereas consonants involve the closure of the wind passage. This, it appears, was very important to the Hebrews. Breath for them possessed an intensely spiritual quality. Much evidence points to this divine dimension of breath, but a good starting point is to follow the roots of etymology. In the days of Moses, the Hebrews had a single word for both *spirit* and *wind* – the word "*rauch*". Many other ancient and tribal cultures share a similar pattern. To the Navajo Indians of North America, breath was known as "the holy wind". The Sanskrit word "*attman*" signifies *soul* as well as *breath*. Closer to home, the word *spirit* and *respiration* are both rooted in the Latin word "spiritus". And in Genesis, was it not the *breath of life* that God blew into Adam's nostrils?

I came upon a theory that the reason the ancient Hebrews refrained from writing vowels was due to their (the vowels') sacred association with the divine. Vowels were considered too pure to desacrilise in written form (just as the Almighty's name was too holy to utter). It was only the Greeks (who didn't share the Hebrews' religious beliefs) who saw fit to add vowels to the written word.[5]

At first all of these insights didn't seem to have much bearing on my Quest. But then I stumbled upon the fact that besides vowels and consonants, there existed a third, smaller group of three letters in its own special category. Although these letters were considered consonants, in certain situations they could also serve as vowels: W H and Y! The uncanny coinciding of these three letters in the Tetragamaton has not gone unnoticed and there is a respected school of thought that believes that the semi-holy quality of the letters (by virtue of their being semi-vowels) is the exact reason that they are contained in the Tetragamaton.

Of the three, it is Y that has most closely retained its vowel status. The only English words that exist today without vowels are those that contain Ys (e.g. sky, fly and why). This is significant because it finally secures this enigmatic letter a unique role among the 26 letters of our alphabet. And this role was about to lead me to one of the greater breakthroughs of my Quest.

[5] Unbeknown to many, even in Greece the vowels retained their holy status. Most people regard the Alpha and the Omega as the first and last letters of the Greek alphabet, but in fact they are more importantly the first and last **vowels** of the Greek alphabet.

Duality

By now my study at home had been transformed into a fully-fledged philosophical research centre. Books piled up on the desk and across the floor. Old maps, philosophical treatises, dictionaries, encyclopedias, Bibles, and a weighty pile of printouts from sessions on the internet, jostled for space with empty tea cups. On the odd occasion when a staff member came round to the house I would, of course, keep the study securely locked. God only knows what they would have thought if they had caught a glimpse of that room. It looked more like the den of a Middle Eastern terrorist than that of a director of one of the most up-and-coming investment firms in town. Sometimes when I saw the suspicious expression on Kate's face as I sat hunched over my PC tapping away, I wondered if she imagined I was really deep in the throes of an e-love affair, probably with an e-lover of Middle Eastern extraction. Actually, I had to concede, it would sound more normal than admitting to conducting passionate research into the difference between vowels and consonants!

However, what made this vowel/consonant breakthrough notable was that it managed to tie up for me a whole lot of loose ends in a single stroke. Up to that point in my Quest I had philosophically examined several seemingly unrelated topics. At times it might have appeared that twigs, coincidences, nightmares, puns, the letter Y and especially the great Egyptian God, Osiris, had no proper place occupying the same story. But in the letter Y I saw the invisible thread that binds all together. The clue can be found within the twofold nature of the letter: as a consonant and as a vowel. Its distinguishing feature is its *duality*.

Once again, etymology exposed the connection. One day I looked up the word "twig" and found to my surprise that it did, in fact, have deeper reasons for its existence. It shared roots (if you'll pardon the pun) with the words "twice" and "twin". A twig usually connects two smaller branches to a single branch. In this sense a twig also possesses a certain amount of duality. Osiris had been referred to as the Dual God, due to his twofold role of inhabiting two different worlds at the same time. In the same way, Y was the letter that could move freely – like a shaman – between the heavenly world of vowels and the mortal world of consonants! And what about puns? Were they not words that connected dual meanings?

At the time I did not appreciate how deep the roots of dualism spread into the lands of my Quest.

Cartesian Thinking

No discussion of Dualism would be complete without reference to the 17th century French philosopher, René Descartes. It was he who most rigorously exposed the dualism he saw inherent in the universe. Like all good philosophers his central concern was the metaphysical question: "What does it mean to be human?" In his contemplation of this issue, Descartes conducted a series of what have been called "thought experiments". Employing a radically sceptical approach, he decided to doubt the reality of all things in the universe unless they were absolutely irrefutable.

He commenced by attacking perception. Descartes was aware that through his five senses he could perceive an external material world that included his body. He postulated that the perceptions that were reaching his awareness could well be the subject matter of an elaborate dream.[6] How can we be absolutely certain that what we call "life" is not just a dream emanating from some other realm of which we are unaware? When we are in our nightly dreams the world around us appears every bit as real as this world. Could our everyday world not be the dream of another world?

He concluded that the entire external world (including our bodies) could well be as ephemeral as our dreams. At first this scepticism seemed to wipe out the existence of everything in the universe

[6] He also postulated that they could be a deceitful illusion conjured up by an "evil demon".

so that there was nothing left. But in due course a subtle problem arose. The only thing that Descartes could not doubt was that he was doubting, and thus he arrived at his immortal statement that has become the bedrock of modern philosophy: *Cogito, Ergo Sum* – "I think, therefore I am". All may well be a dream and therefore unreal, but you could not refute that there was a dreamer dreaming. Therefore the dreamer had to exist.

This conclusion had far-reaching implications. If everything in the external material world could be non-existent, but thinking could not, it meant that thinking belonged to a world other than the external material world. *In other words there was not one world – but two.* The answer to the question "What does it mean to be human?" is *twofold*. Humans consist of two totally different things: a body, extended in space; and another immaterial substance called mind, which does not occupy space and is not subject to spatial laws. This "two-world" view, in a nutshell, is dualism.

The essential attribute of dualism is that it divides previously undivided areas of life into two sub-areas. The most popular line along which the division takes place usually entails separating mental, immaterial things from material things. Thus we have "mind and matter", "body and soul", and "idealism and materialism". But dualism needn't be restricted to the mind/body relationship. Osiris's "This world" and the "Other world" is an example of dualism that is not strictly divided along the mental/non-mental faultline. Dualism is an underlying pattern rather than a specific association and this pattern lurks in a whole host of structures including religion, science and politics.

Common-sense observation of our own lives and experience confirms that there do seem to be two different types of "ingredients" (for want of a better word) that make up this life. In this respect Cartesian thinking seems to be a pretty accurate description of the way things are.

However dualism has a critical problem. We know from everyday life that mind and body definitely interact with each other. The mind affects the body all of the time; if you have the thought to stand up then (provided you are able to), your body stands up. By the same token, ingesting hallucinogenic drugs into the body has an effect on the mind. But in this interaction is exactly where dualism's problem lies. For, how can two "ingredients" which belong to two such different worlds interact with each other? How can something that is immaterial exercise any force on that which is material? How do the two interface?

Descartes tried to rescue dualism from this gaping disparity by stating that the point of contact between mind and body occurred at the pineal gland, which resides in the brain. However, this claim was fraught with its own contradictions, for Descartes had categorically stated that the mind, being an immaterial substance, was not subject to spatial laws. If it was not subject to spatial laws how could you, then, even talk of "point of contact"? "Point of contact" is a spatial concept. Not surprisingly, Descartes' philosophy of dualism has been disparaged by philosophers ever since.

Nevertheless, dualistic thinking created a chasm that no western philosopher has managed to bridge. To this day humankind finds itself precariously straddled between two logically incompatible worlds. There seems somewhere, in the make up of the universe, to be a vital missing link.

The Pythagorean Letter

Not only was there a missing link in the universe. Any link that there had been between my moonlighting and daylight activities was disappearing at an atrocious speed. By day I would be advising clients on the merits of "top-down asset allocation strategies to accumulate and conserve wealth", but by night I was starting to believe that perhaps this Questor was destined to become some sort of offbeat mystic.

the wor d

the world

the world

the world

the world

the missing link ©

THE MISSING INK

I've been talking quite casually about quests so far, but historically the true quest is a very serious undertaking. All quests share a common purpose – the search for some mystical object or thing. It is essential that the Questor who embarks on such a search possess an undying belief in the divine power of this mystical object, and an understanding that finding the object will solve all of life's unfathomable riddles. In the Middle Ages it was the elusive Holy Grail for which the gallant knight set out into uncharted territories. To embark on such a quest was the most virtuous journey that a man could take and success (con***quest***) was often a matter of life and death. The Philosopher's Stone is another enigmatic treasure that has been sought by countless seekers over the ages. What the exact object of my Quest was, I was still not entirely certain, but I too had a stubborn belief that if I found it, it would solve all of my unanswered questions.

Despite this mystical heritage, I was to find the richest of clues in the places where I least expected them. I was sitting in my offices one morning, contemplating the direction of the Nikkei stock market, when I stumbled upon a crucial piece of information. As a matter of routine I would read the morning newspaper, working backwards from the financial section. Towards the end of the Classifieds there were always a few daily comic strips, one of them titled "Word for Word". This strip portrayed, in a comical way, the etymology of everyday words. Out of pure curiosity my reading routine included glancing at this comic strip. I was invariably disappointed, though, with the trivial nature of the words chosen and I harboured a secret conviction that, had I been given such an etymological platform to commandeer, I would have done a far superior job of enlightening the reading public.

But on this particular morning the comic strip etymologist displayed a stroke of absolute genius. For there, only five pages north of the Nikkei stockmarket slump, was the most valuable etymology of the letter Y that I have come across to date. "The letter Y," it said "is sometimes called the letter of Pythagoras... as a symbol of the diverging paths of good and evil". I immediately abandoned the Japanese economy and dived into the internet where *google.com* revealed a whole host of related links to "Pythagorean letter".

When Kate found out that I was researching Pythagoras she became exasperated. "First Egyptian gods, then French philosophers and now Greek mathematicians! I swear that you've lost it. It's all just escapism... Pipe dreams..."
"But Kate, you have to admit, things are getting a little better. Can't you see that the depression has started to lift?"
"OK," she conceded, frowning, "but that's thanks to the Prozac – not these weird theories of yours".
"And the nightmares? What about those? They've also slowed down. You have to admit it. It can't *all* be the Prozac..."

I pressed on with Pythagoras, the legendary Greek philosopher and mathematician who lived in 500 BC. Many academics regard him as the founder of mathematics and, although he is not given the same philosophic status as Plato or Aristotle, no true account of the origin of western philosophy can afford to bypass Pythagoras.

His principal area of interest was geometry and he had an intense fascination with shapes and numerical ratios. It was he who uttered the immortal words, "All is number". But his fascination stretched even further than the confines of scientific thinking, for he believed that shapes and numbers contained within them the deepest secrets of the universe. Believing that he was a divinely gifted interpreter of these secrets, he formed a religious sect with his followers and Pythagorean philosophy was only practised on a clandestine basis within this sect's confines. As a result, much of the great thinker's legacy is shrouded in mystery, and separating fact from myth is no easy task.

amily are Malawians. – IPS

WORD FOR WORD

There is no doubt, though, that Pythagoras had a special association with the letter Y. Some believe that the Y shape was used as a central symbol in Pythagorean initiation ceremonies. Others believe that Pythagoras renamed himself with a secret name commencing with a Y, a name known only to his followers. There is even a fair sized school of thought that believes that Pythagoras personally invented the letter and added it to his contemporary alphabet (hence the "Pythagorean letter").

The only really indisputable evidence that I managed to glean on this mystical association, I found in a historical poem written by the renowned Roman poet of Pythagoras's era, Virgil:

> *The Pythagoric letter two way spread,*
> *shows the two paths in which man's life is led.*
> *The right hand to sacred virtue tends,*
> *though steep and rough at first, in rest it ends:*
> *The other broad and smooth but from its crown,*
> *on rocks the traveler is tumbled down.*
> *He who to virtue by harsh toils aspires,*
> *subduing pains, worth and renown acquires:*
> *but who seeks slothful luxury, and flies*
> *the labour of great acts dishonoured dies.*

At the time of reading them, I wasn't aware that these words would hold the final clue to my question "*Why?*". But after ruminating over the verse for a few evenings a significant pattern began to emerge; a pattern that, in retrospect, was literally the "shape of things to come". The Pythagoric letter symbolised a *dilemma*. This was the starting point.

Pythagoras had identified the dualistic nature of life way before Descartes. His division of life into "*the two paths in which man's life is led*" reflects an equally powerful dualism, one that has been with us since the Garden of Eden: the problem of good and evil. Just as Adam and Eve were faced with the Tree of Knowledge of good and evil, the Pythagorean was faced with a choice between two paths, a choice between the two arms of the letter Y.

What made Pythagoras's approach to dualism unique is that inherent in the Pythagorean letter was a split in the road; more specifically an *either/or* split. *Either* you went the one way, *or* you went the other. A choice had to be made to the inclusion of one and the exclusion of the other.

Double Bind

To the Pythagoreans there was not much moral latitude in the either/or split. Choosing the virtuous path and excluding the path of luxury was the obvious choice. But what happens when the choice is not that straightforward? What happens when your Master says, "Do not eat of the tree for if you do you will die", but you are starving and there are no other trees in sight? Then a friendly serpent says, "Try it, it'sssss delicioussss and you will not die". Your mind knows that you should never disobey the Master, but your body knows that it has to get some food. *Either* you listen to your mind, refrain from eating the fruit and risk dying of hunger *or* you listen to your body and eat of the fruit and risk disobeying your Master. Both have positives and negatives. Each could seem equally attractive. You are then, as they say, "on the horns of a dilemma". *The letter Y is a dilemma.*

"A dilemma," I mused, one Sunday afternoon, sitting snugly in the armchair in my study, a copy of Virgil's poem on one side, my dictionaries, and books on philosophy and psychology, on the other. That morning, I'd been researching two words of interest to my Quest: "Schizophrenia" and "individual". The etymology is pretty straightforward, I'd found. "Schizophrenia" shares the same root as "schism" and literally means "split mind". The message in "individual's" etymology is less direct, but equally important. Individual stems from the Latin "individuus", meaning "undivided".

DUALISM

Rain drummed steadily on the wooden decking outside as I contemplated these meanings. My eye fell idly once again on Virgil's poem: "The Pythagoric letter two way spread..." In time to the rain, I drummed my fingers on the arm of the chair. Something was bothering me; a feeling of familiarity; a faint recollection of something similar I myself might once have written. I leapt up, determined to see if I was right.

In the spare room was a mess of old boxes and suitcases, holding artifacts from my past. Kate often despaired over the spare room, not only over the dilapidated appearance of the storage containers but also my need to store old stuff. (One of her best friends had taken one look around the door and declared, to Kate's great amusement, "Chris is sabotaging your *Feng Shui* with all this unfinished business; there's way too much Yin in this room!") Now, I waded through box after box. Dust clogged my throat and tickled my eyes. I had to clear a monster cobweb from the corner, and I dragged a dusty trunk out into the passage to make more space. Kate began to get highly annoyed, as we had guests coming over that evening. "You're messing up the house with these damn stupid adventures! Can't you just restrict them to that study of yours?"

I hardly heard her, because... I'd found it! There it lay, yellowed and crumpled among some other papers. My poem. Not 2000 years old, but a mere fifteen. Not written by an illustrious poet, but by an amateur. However, within its lines can clearly be discerned the echo of what Virgil was saying (even though Virgil's "Pythagoric letter" was not even known to exist by the amateur poet when he wrote):

> I'm going to tell you a tale
> Of a train that went off the rails
> Everything was going fine
> Until I reached the time
> When I reached an intersection

And had to choose a direction
The one road was hard
Barren and untarred
The other road had crowds
And led up into the clouds
Was I going to travel
Through all the ruts and gravel?
Or was I going to cruise
With all the drugs and booze?
Was I a go-getter
A trendy jet-setter?
Or was I just mellow
A quiet, content fellow?
Which route should I follow?
Where would I be tomorrow?
Unfortunately I lacked the precision
To make such a decision
So one part of me went one way
And the other part went a bit stray
As the days went by, each part
Grew further and further apart
We seem to have lost each other forever
When will I be together?

The poem I'd written in the month following my release from Ward 24.

At the time that I wrote it, I had had no idea of any deeper meaning in the words I scribbled on the page. I had been depressed and disoriented, and had churned out a lot of jumbled poetry[7] at that stage.

The poem provided the bridge between the letter Y and what had happened fifteen years earlier. Was my poem not essentially about a *dilemma*, and the inability to solve this dilemma? Had this inability not led to a split occurring, so that the individual

---

[7] A larger collection of these poems can be seen on the author's website: **www.thewordproject.com**

could no longer retain the condition of "undividedness"? Was the state of "split mind" (or Schizophrenia) not inevitable after that? Was the branch in the professor's office not only a symbol for coincidences, puns and dilemmas – but a perfect symbol for Schizophrenia?

One of the predominant environmental causes of Schizophrenia is the exposure of the individual to what is called "*the double bind*". The double bind is essentially a dilemma. It occurs when an individual (usually a child) is faced with two competing messages that carry contradictory meanings. A simple example would be when a parent jokingly says to a child, "You can't have that!" while at the same time smiling at the child in such a way as to convey that the child *can* have it. Normally the child would be able to work through such a dilemma, but in certain situations (especially when there is gross over-exposure to double binds) the child gets stuck on the dilemma.

They lack the precision,
to make such a decision,
so the one part goes one way,
and the other part goes a bit stray.

The mind splits.

"Ambivalence" is another technical term prevalent in the literature on Schizophrenia. This is a characteristic trait of Schizophrenics and manifests in their harbouring contradictory emotions for the same person or object (e.g. simultaneously loving and hating the same person). As a result, Schizophrenics often respond to situations with seemingly inappropriate emotions. A word that shares its stem with "ambiguity" is ambivalence, "ambi" denoting "two ways". So ambivalence is simply the unresolved double bind *internalised.* It is an either/or that cannot be resolved – a Y junction that is impassable.

Ratio-nality

"You're spending less and less time at the office, Chris. Surely it can't be good for business. You're going to start losing clients. The whole reason you started Prozac was because your business was being affected by your depression. But now you spend even less time at the office. You're going to regret it – I'm telling you."

The dilemma that I had faced prior to my hospitalisation in 1984 was not simply a matter of choosing between being "a trendy jet-setter", and being a "quiet, content fellow". It was a dilemma whose cracks, I am beginning to realise, spread deep into the foundations of the society in which I was living at the time.

We westerners do not realise how integral the concept of "division" is to our way of thinking. Division can be found in every sphere of our intellectual lives. Long before Descartes bisected the universe into material things and immaterial things, the ancient Greeks had been at work dividing up everything they could get their hands on. Western science has often been called analytical science; the word *analysis* has Greek origins and means "to break things apart". And that is exactly what they did in Athens back in 400 BC. Having divided everything up into ever-smaller divisions, the Greeks eventually reached what they believed was an indivisible entity and this they called the atom (from the Greek "indivisible"). The wise men who "discovered" the atom promptly named themselves the Atomists, and became the leading scientific and philosophic community of their time. (Perhaps it would have been better for humankind if later generations of scientists had taken the Greek's word for it about the atom being indivisible. Instead, during the course of the last century, some brilliant scientists managed to split the atom itself, leaving us with our legacy of planet-threatening nuclear stockpiles.)

Mathematicians too have been very busy with division over the past 2000 years. They started out with the Natural numbers, which were great for addition and multiplication, but inadequate for any other mathematical operations. Thus they developed the Integers so that they could expand into the field of subtraction. But, still this wasn't enough, and it was only when they had developed the *Rational* numbers, that they could apply that most esteemed of algebraic manipulations – division. Once again *the spell is in the spelling*. The word "rational" takes its root from the word "ratio". How do you get a ratio? By *dividing* a whole into parts.

Less obvious is the fact that "ratio" is also the root for both "rational" (as in sane) and "reason", (that demi-god of western thought for which I had been so desperately searching). *Does this congruity suggest that implicit in rational, reasonable, sane thinking lurks an element of division?* Or is this just another "arbitrary" relationship?[8]

(One relationship that I feared might be destined for the "arbitrary" pile was that between Kate and me. The physical attraction between us was still there, no doubt about that, although she increasingly complained that we didn't spend enough time together, "being romantic". But were our minds not parting ways? In the beginning we'd both tried (and I the more so, I think) to conform to each others' "standards" and it was only now, a year later, that our true selves (my true self?) was beginning to emerge. That's what's wrong with courtship. It's the old PR department problem again: "Bombard them with adverts, bombard them with lies, coat them in sugar, a slick disguise…" As I sat and contemplated *division*, I decided to push personal relationship doubts to the very back of my mind…)

Division, I realised, is not confined to science. It is also to be found happily ensconced in the backyard of science's age-old arch-rival: religion. If anything, the Judeo-Christian faith is even more dependent than science on dualism. Its very foundations are structured on the dualities of good and evil, salvation and damnation, heaven and earth, God and the devil. The "forces of

---

[8] And is it a coincidence that the devil's number can be derived directly from one of the most fundamental of ratios? 2:1 = 0,666

light versus the forces of darkness" is the central theme of the whole show, the Tree of Knowledge of good and evil being the grand-daddy of all dilemmas!

The Bible is none other than a chronicle of the almighty war between the forces of good and the forces of evil. It is not a book of serenity and peace, but a story of battles and conflict, struggle and toil. Not surprising then that today, far from being the land of milk and honey, the Promised Land is a region of escalating death and bloodshed. It has been suggested by many a Christian that, "Hell must be to know that there is no God". I think it's a matter of perspective; if my experience in Ward 24 taught me anything, it was that, "*Heaven is to know that there is no devil*!"

Divide and Conquer

Until I embarked on this philosophical search I was unaware of how deeply polarity is woven into the very fabric of western society. Unless you take time out to Stop, Look and Listen, the extent of the division can go unremarked. In fact, though, I am now certain that it was *division*, more than anything else, that caused 1984.

The world that I inhabited back then was far more divided than today. Society was fraught with fault lines. After all, it was a period in history known as the Bi-polar era[9] and there was no more fitting symbol of the division than the Berlin Wall which stretched some 45 km between East and West Germany. It was the Cold War – Communism versus Capitalism – and a mighty iron curtain ensured that nobody would cross the either/or divide.

In that same year several thousand miles south of Berlin was a political system that had taken the either/or dichotomy to its practical extreme. According to the South African regime of the day, you were *either* white *or* you were non-white (black) and the whole political structure of apartheid endeavoured to ensure that nobody crossed this line. In this system inclusion and

[9] Perhaps it is no coincidence that manic depression, a scourge of our times, is called "Bi-polar" depression.

exclusion were implemented by force. “Apart” was the active ingredient of apartheid and division was its *modus operandi.*

Unlike in Berlin, apartheid wasn’t about Western European against Eastern European. It was far more serious. It was about white versus black, about “civilisation” versus “savagery”, about the so-called forces of light against the forces of darkness. And apartheid wasn’t, as the rest of the western world liked to think, a new invention. When Julius Caesar proclaimed “Divide and Conquer!” he launched an imperial tradition that would last for 2000 years. In Australia, America, and the east, the pattern had been the same; the Imperialist European Christian versus the indigenous native pagan. And in every instance the scientific technology of the alien Europeans smashed the fragile resistance of the local peoples (who were generally an intuitive and artistic community and less developed in terms of western conceptions of scientific advancement).

I am not the only white South African who today looks back at my childhood and asks, “Did we really have that system? Were there really two signs outside every public toilet and in front of every queue?” It almost has a surreal element now and yet I can remember the signs very vividly, one for “Whites” and one for “Non-Whites”. And where there was only *one* park bench, or *one* golden beach, an imperious “Net Blankes” – “Whites Only”. A big part of our childhood landscape. It was always “Us” and “Them”, them being the great threatening “Other”, the forces of darkness that were constantly threatening to contaminate our “pure” white blood.

Up until high school I never really questioned anything. A model pupil. Top of my class. So immersed in my schoolbooks that what went on in the outside world didn’t really concern me – things just *were* the way they were. Even if I had developed the whim to look outwards, I wouldn't have seen much further than the borders of that wonderful cocoon in which we all lived –

upper-class, exclusively-white suburbia. Besides the odd "native boy" or "native girl" cleaning some part of our property we might just as well have been living in Holland or England.

On reaching high school, things changed a little. For some reason, (probably the proximity of an overbearing and extremely rigid father) the teenage rebellion thing kicked in really hard with me. Out went the schoolbooks and in came the dope smoking, dropping out and general non-conformity. All authority figures were targets of dissent, and the apartheid government was one of them.

In those turbulent years I ventured a little further out of my comfortable white world. The "native-boys" were the ones who supplied us with our stash of *dagga*. We all became quite friendly. We'd often have smoking sessions together and sometimes on Sundays we would even go along to a black soccer match and mingle with our "brothers". And we certainly badmouthed the apartheid government and the police force (particularly the latter because of the constant fear of getting "caught in possession").

It was trendy in those days to listen to reggae and we swore allegiance to our Rastafarian brothers from Jamaica. When Jimmy Cliff came to Durban in 1980, we crowded into King's Park stadium with thousands of black people, clouds of sweet *dagga* smoke billowing in the floodlights. In my final year of school, I did my history project on the injustices of Slavery, and my English Oral on the music of Bob Marley. In a more daring moment I even spray-painted the words "Equal Rights and Justice" in big letters across the road in front of my parents' home.

But despite all these token acts of "political resistance", I cannot honestly say that I had sleepless nights over apartheid. Or that I would gladly have traded my R 400 Levi's with the worn trousers of one of my black brothers. Rather, I had found myself a niche in my all-white high school in which being anti-apartheid was pretty trendy. The wrongs of apartheid niggled my conscience, certainly, but I was unaware all the while of the destructive groundwork that this ever-present division was performing on my psyche.

A Stormy Passage

Closer to home I had an even more menacing division to deal with. Actually, "closer to home" is not entirely accurate because the division I am talking about took place *in* my home. I have already mentioned the conflict in my parent's marriage, but what I haven't explained is that this conflict was demarcated, I'd argue, along the exact same lines as apartheid.

It was my father, the arrogant and linear scientist, exercising imperial control over my mother, the emotional artist. It was the rational and enlightened powers of reason and logic, against the dark, murky forces of art and myth. It was the organised and structured versus the spontaneous and flowing. Just as the marauding Europeans' superior weaponry had conquered the darker skinned, weaker communities into submission all over the world, my own mother lived in the shadow of my father's oppression for as long as I can remember.

Never a day went by without an argument, never a night without a barrage of scathing comments. But what was perhaps worse than the shouting and cursing was the lack of love. If, during my entire childhood, I witnessed one hug between my parents, or one instance where they held hands, I must confess that I don't remember it. This was marital schism at its worst.

I do not hold my parents responsible for 1984. If you could scapegoat your parents for your own life, my father could well scapegoat his parents for his. I have no doubt that both my mother and father always loved my sister and me wholeheartedly. We were always very important to them and both of them made considerable sacrifices for us over the years. If anything, the reason that they never divorced (which in my opinion they should have) was because they stayed together for our sakes. But the fact that my sister suffered for nearly a decade from a severe eating disorder is evidence of the damage that schisms can cause.

Perhaps I would not be so forgiving of my parent's marriage had I not come to realise (via this Quest) that the conflict and dilemma contained in their relationship was simply the playing out of a far greater schism in society. There are countless marriages where the same old patriarchal patterns are played out. And, invariably, the role-players are not even aware of the sinister forces of dualism directing the play.

The minute I finished school, I bolted from the family home. I was only seventeen at the time but, on pretence of being nineteen, managed to secure a job as a cocktail barman at a casino 200 km south of Durban. The bar I manned overlooked a flock of roulette tables and from where I served my concoctions I could see the "jet-setters" throwing their money around.

I received my call-up papers to report for compulsory military conscription in July that year, but being as opposed to authority and as unenthusiastic about defending apartheid as I was, I knew that somehow I had to evade the call-up. A friend and I had seen an ad looking for crewmen for a round-the-world yacht trip. On 7 July that year, seven days after I was meant to report for military duty, we left Durban harbour in a 34-foot yacht headed for Cape Town and then the Caribbean. Technically I was on AWOL, but I had R 900 in my pocket and the world was my oyster.

I never got as far as Cape Town. It turned out that the skipper had never sailed a yacht at sea before. Halfway between Durban and East London, on a notorious piece of coastline known as the Wild Coast, we hit an almighty storm. I still remember the crackling and distorted weather report being read out slowly, word by word, on Channel 16 of our tiny radio set: "All ships……All ships……we……have….a…..gale warning…."

With a full day's sail in either direction to get to the nearest port, we were sitting ducks. Waves the size of small mountains bore down on us and at about 11 that night, exasperated, the skipper popped about five sleeping tablets and said, "See you guys in the morning!"

Ten days later, by which time we had passed through another two storms, I decided that the army would be a better bet. I was painfully aware that the skipper still had not proceeded past Chapter One of his book on basic sextant use, our only means of navigation. On one occasion he actually sent two of us paddling in to shore on surfboards to "find out where we are"! I decided there and then that I would rather entrust my life to some racist Sergeant Major.

Six months later, 10 January 1983, I waved bye-bye to my civilian friends and walked through the gates of the South African Defence Force. I had been allocated to the First Mechanised Infantry Division. On that day I was still unaware of the sinister forces lurking within that word "Division".

Division in the Ranks

Basics training was a nightmare! My training camp was based in Bloemfontein, and the overwhelming memory is of *brown*! Our uniforms were brown. Our boots were brown. Our parade grounds were brown. Our underpants were brown. Hell, even the covers of the miniature Bibles they issued us were brown. I spent three months being screamed and shouted at by horrible looking Afrikaners with moustaches. Our bodies were pushed to breaking point. I felt like I was in prison. In retrospect, did we even have as many rights as prisoners had? Probably not! We were the property of the Pretoria regime, and they could treat us as they wished.

Surprisingly, I managed to cope fairly well with the first six months of army training. I absolutely loathed it, but I coped. My body got fit fairly quickly and I kept a low profile. After Second Phase training my Lieutenant even offered to recommend me for Officer Training, but to his amazement I declined. Instead, I jumped at the opportunity when it was announced that a special platoon of dedicated drivers was required for urgent border duty. I figured that being a driver would be a damn sight better than being a Rifleman. But more importantly, I *had* to get out of that training camp. Within a month we were in the midst of the steaming stupor of Central Africa. (Most people consider Angola as Southern Africa, but on a map it is closer to Central Africa.)

After fifteen years I have forgotten the nature of exactly what was going on deep inside of me at that point. The reason I can't remember is that there seemed almost to be an internal silence in place during that period. The silence had an unnatural quality in itself, almost – dare I say – the sound of suppression. The lines of division had long been drawn out in the sands of my soul, and if I had known better at the time, I would have recognised in the silence the same soundlessness that falls over armies preparing for war. I had tried my hardest to escape from all the dilemmas in my life. In resigning myself to the fact that escape was not an option, I guess that deep down I knew that war was the only alternative.

On the trip into Angola, a stroke of bad luck placed me in the driver's seat of an armoured car that carried five of the most vulgar, barbaric people I have ever met. They were Afrikaners in their late twenties (ten years my senior) and had been hand picked for their frontline battle experience in previous Angolan operations. They took an instant dislike to me and in the days that followed this mutual dislike intensified into a deep-seated hatred. I was the young rookie Englishman from Durban and they were the hardened *Boere*. I was the *sout-piel*, with one leg in Africa and the other in Britain, and my penis (*piel*) hanging in the salty (*sout*) Atlantic Ocean. Over the next few weeks all of the hatred between Boer and Brit that had supposedly been buried after the Anglo-Boer War, reared its ugly head in our platoon.

I was stuck with them for four months. Four months. I remember the excruciatingly slow moving conveys that would last for days and nights at a time, crawling across the dry African scrub. On one particular convoy I had driven for a fifty-hour stretch without sleep. Drivers had to concentrate fiercely to dodge the constant potholes where enemy landmines were placed. We were often reminded that the heavily reinforced steel that surrounded us became as pliant as a Coke can in the grip of a landmine. RPG rockets were to be even more feared as they could rip into the guts of an armoured vehicle, causing total carnage inside.

All the while a constant barrage of insults flowed from the back of the armoured car. It was "them" against "me" and, at five to one, the odds were far from even! Just before we crossed the border into Angola, a timid looking Lance Corporal was assigned to our vehicle. I hoped the presence of rank would calm things down. But the *Ou Manne*[10] were all over him and it was only a matter of hours before it could be seen who was really in control of that vehicle. The deeper we got into Angola, the worse things became.

One day the biggest, nastiest looking of the *Ou Manne* pushed me off the roof of a building and I was knocked unconscious when I struck the hard ground some eight feet below. A Captain rushed me to the medics' tent and that afternoon I was told to lie down and keep quiet. The *Ou Manne* had made the whole thing look like an accident and the incident was soon forgotten. (I wasn't the only driver who had a rough time of it – one night a fellow rookie driver was smacked over the back of his head with the butt of a "passenger's" rifle.)

---

[10] The Afrikaans translation of "Old Men", used in the SADF to refer to soldiers who had been in the army for longer than a year.

Every now and then I was sure that I detected a hint of sympathy from the Lance Corporal. But he was powerless. The closer you get to the enemy, the wilder things get and the less rank counts.

One day in Southern Angola I wandered alone through the bombed out remains of what had been a small village. We had pitched camp nearby and were allowed some time on our own. There was carnage everywhere and the streets were littered with mangled belongings. The bank deposit slips of a former Portuguese General Dealer fluttering aimlessly down the main street… The burnt out wreckage of a tank with the words NAO AJUDA painted on the sides… A pit full of discarded medicine ampoules… Swedish sardine tins… Another pit full of charred human bones and skeletons… An abandoned rag doll with a leg missing… The tattered menu from a local eating house.

In one burnt out building I came across piles and piles of papers scattered on the floor. Mostly they were business records but among them were hundreds of pamphlets expounding the virtues of Marxism. Here and there I saw a one pager with an ominous looking skull and crossbones on the front and a warning written in three languages: the local population should evacuate the area before the bombing began.

In one corner of the building a small fluttering piece of green paper caught my eye. It was a poem, written in a simple fashion, dedicated to a freedom fighter. I still remember some of the words…

Stand tall O freedom fighter
Stand proud amongst your brothers
You alone give us hope
As they kill our sons and mothers…

The words touched me and I stood there for what must have been a full minute staring intently at the piece of paper.

In looking back, if there was one moment that captured the dilemma of the whole SADF experience for me, it was that moment, reading the poem of the enemy. For deep within I intuitively knew that the words of this poem were beautiful and that the real enemy that I faced was the *Ou Manne*. This was the double bind – the Y shaped branch that pierced my conscience. I stuffed the poem into the inner of my metal helmet, making sure nobody saw me.[11] That night sleep evaded me as I stared up at the stars from my shallow trench.

And so, in Angola, I came up against the same problem that I had experienced my whole life: *internal division*. It wasn't only the war outside of our camp that was causing me problems; it was the war within. The *division in the ranks*. Civil unrest, like cancer, weakens the system from within. That is where my problems always lay – *within* my country, *within* my society, *within* my family and now *within* my platoon. Only now, looking back, could I see that such a long line of "withins" would inevitably lead to the ultimate war: the war within my*self*. The enemy was not without – *the enemy was within*.

A Question Answered

Despite the tremendous strain and stress that I endured in Angola, I managed to survive, and by October of 1983 I had returned to my old training camp in Bloemfontein. I was determined to get back to my hometown, Durban, and by contriving an elaborate request, which played heavily on an old back injury sustained in childhood, I secured the most coveted of infantry camp prizes – a transfer to Natal Command.

The day I packed my bags and bade farewell to the dusty brown grounds of Bloemfontein must rank as one of the best days of my life. And, until that Friday night when I lay on the back seat of my car in the dark driveway of my parents' home, my few short months at Natal Command were among the happiest times of my life. I had conquered the ultimate of the authority figures

[11] I had to leave the poem in Angola as I would have been in serious trouble if the military had ever found it in my possession.

in my life, the First South African Mechanised Division. Little did I know then that another, more sinister, division lurked within...

By the time the notorious Friday evening in March 1984 arrived, in retrospect it was entirely appropriate that I had a vision of *two* of me. For there *were* two of me! It was not only my moment of *vision* but more significantly my moment of *di*vision! Neither is it surprising that the one self I saw was white and the other black. This was a perfectly sane manifestation of the division I had been living with for most of my life: good versus evil; white versus black; Dad versus Mom; science versus art; organised versus spontaneous; rational versus irrational.

And on the first day I'd entered hospital, what was the list that I had been mysteriously possessed to place in the middle of my bed? The list with day, Adam, positive and white on the one side, and night, Eve, negative and black on the other? Was this not my instinctive recognition of the division that was tearing my life apart?

Was it not the suppressed, marginalised part of myself that had been suddenly awakened "as if from a deep slumber" by the penetrating call of the Muezzin that Friday afternoon on the motorbike? Was this not the darker, misunderstood self, the self that had always been oppressed, like my mom had been; like South Africa's black people had been? Was my moment of division not the internal revolt of a faction that had been subdued for too long?

Was it not this newly awakened, darker self who had been so obsessed with superstition and mystical meaning? Was this new self not the "*other part*" that "*went a bit stray*"; the part that rebelled against the rational, scientific, western worldview? Was there some profound and prophetic truth in the Bible verse: "I urge you my brothers, watch out for those who cause divisions and upset people's faith"?

DIVISION ©

**DOUBLE VISION
SECOND SIGHT?**

And what about the Alpha and the Omega? Would it not make sense for a person whose very sanity was threatened by division to spend hours and hours trying to re-unite these two extremes? Could such a person not instinctively believe that in rejoining these almighty symbols and thereby transcending the double bind, he could somehow put his own Humpty Dumpty together again?

And what of this Quest, this obsession with finding a joining link between word and world; between the apparently unrelated incidents in a coincidence; between the dual meanings of a pun? Could this not also be considered a desperate – and quite sane – attempt to heal a severely fractured and insane world?

Finally, to my great relief, I had found my answer to the question "*Why*"? And perhaps more importantly, I had found the wisdom contained in that branch of wood that the night-time stranger had delivered into my life.

* * *

"Come talk to me Chris, we haven't chatted since I got home. In fact, you know," she says playfully, "we haven't chatted for ages!"

"I'm sorry, Darling, I'm busy."

She sticks her head around the study door and observes me settled in the armchair in the corner. I feel a bit guilty when I see her hurt eyes and pinched mouth.

"Busy? … What're you busy doing? Looks to me like you're just sitting there." She adds, sarcastically, "How unusual". We'd been down this road before. Many times. "How many times do I have to defend my right to think, Kate. I'm busy thinking."

"Thinking, thinking, thinking. Always bloody thinking! Maybe sometime you can sit there and think about us!" The door slams.

Her normally light footsteps can be heard thudding angrily down the carpeted corridor. I sigh, and reach wearily for my cup of ginger and honey tea.

I hear her footsteps approaching again. The door flies open. “Oh, and if you do decide to think about us any time, please be sure to let me know – I’d hate to miss out on that rare moment of togetherness!”

The door slams again.

Outside, far across the twilight valley, I hear the call of a fiery-necked nightjar: “Good Lord Deliver Us”.

part III

THE WAY

Abide not with dualism
Carefully avoid pursuing it;
As soon as you have right and wrong
Confusion ensues and the Way is lost…

…Forget the wherefore of things,
and we attain to a state beyond analogy.

On Believing in Mind – Seng-t'san

Concatenation
"Bhutan? But why on earth do you want to go there?" She's incredulous.
"I've just got this feeling, Kate. Call it a premonition. Call it a hunch – I have to go."
"A *hunch*? A goddamned hunch? I can hardly believe this latest madness! So you're proposing to leave your business, to leave me, to jeopardise everything, for the sake of a *hunch*?" The argument had moved out of the study now and into the lounge.
"Okay, so it's more than a hunch – it's part of my research. Think of it as a field trip."
She folds her slim arms militantly across her front. "And besides," she demands, looking rather comical I think, "where exactly do *I* fit in on your list of priorities? Probably slotted in between your precious Y and Z in one of your more obscure alphabets". She was starting to rave. Soon she'd be ranting about marriage and how weird her friends were starting to find me and other unpalatable subjects. This was not going to be easy. She was reacting far worse than I'd expected. But there was no alternative – I had to go to Bhutan.

* * *

A true quest never ends. That is because a quest is more of a journey than a destination and the concept of "arrival" would be a contradiction. Only in finite realms can you reach ends, and as the greatest quests are ultimately more concerned with infinite matters, the concept of beginnings and ends is an anomaly.

Knowing *why* a person has contracted Schizophrenia doesn't necessarily cure the Schizophrenia. Knowing *why* Humpty Dumpty fell off the wall isn't much going to help the king's men to put him together again. Despite not having had a nightmare about forked branches for nearly a month, I still had a strong sense of something missing. I still had not found what I was looking for.

Besides, there were still some seemingly less important questions that I had not solved. The branch in the professor's office was directly related to division and Schizophrenia. But how had it come to be there? The verse on divisions from the Bible was quite probably the most relevant verse that I could have chosen from the Bible. But I *hadn't* chosen it, so who had? And while we are on the topic, how did I know, ten years before it had come about, that South Africa would be called a "Rainbow Nation"?

In what is becoming a ritual these days, Kate shakes her head, wearily, a helpless look on her face, "You know, Chris, I don't get it. I really don't. You're going beyond *reason*!" I look at her sharply. "Katie, my darling," I smile, trying desperately to connect with her, "I'll take that as a compliment". My retort seems only to make her more irritated.

It's true, though; I found what she said interesting, because in a sense she was spot-on. I *was* going beyond reason. I had started to know instinctively that reason was not going to give me the answers. I was dealing here with something "beyond the rational" and it was becoming clear that asking "*Why*?" was not going to shed any further light. My discovery of reason's subversive link with the word "division" (via ratio) had left me uncomfortable with it and I realised that I had come to the end of reason's road. From here on, I was going to need something else to guide my Quest.

For a while I floundered, unsure where to find this new guiding light. In our modern world we are so used to the powers of the intellect being able to solve all, that once reason is rendered powerless we find ourselves adrift on unknown seas without a map. At one point I even considered the possibility that there are some things that just can't be known, and maybe it would be just as well to "let sleeping dogs lie". But I knew that such an approach was not going to take away the terrible *angst* that had surfaced in my life; one day I would have to come off the

Prozac and the *angst* would be ten times worse.

"Look, Chris, I'm not trying to be funny…"
"But …?" I add sarcastically.
She tries again: "It's not like I'm not sympathetic or anything, what you went through, you know, back then. But how the hell can it help you to go delving into all this obscure stuff: linguistics, and history, and codes? Have you considered it might be more effective to rather just *avoid* all this, to stop baffling your brain, to focus on being positive for a change? On doing fun things?"

I feel irritated. Hurt. Misunderstood. It's true, I can't easily justify the strategy I've adopted for fighting meaninglessness. But it does seem to make sense. My "empirical data" would have to be that I feel less despairing these days, more energised and alive.

She continues, trying not to sound nasty I suppose, "I mean, Chris, after all these months, what have you got? What have *we* got? We never even spend any time together".

Kate's still looking at me, quizzically, expecting an answer, but I am already thinking of other things.

It's easy to doubt yourself at such times, but I was not about to admit defeat. I instinctively clutched at the letter Y – the only tangible thing I had. After all, it was this symbol, more than anything else, that had consistently nudged me in the right direction. I figured to myself, "If I keep the Y central, and follow my enquiry where it takes me, I am sure I will find some pointers". Maybe, I puzzled, there was a further link between the development of the letter Y, and the real world? I had already unearthed the Hebrew Yod, and the Pythagoric Letter; maybe there was something else lurking in the mists of time?

Between Pythagoras, Byblos and the Hebrews I seemed to have

run out of fresh leads on the shores of the Mediterranean. It was for this reason that I turned to the east. Somewhere in my readings I had learnt that in China (unlike in the western world), rather than being random or arbitrary the alphabet was firmly grounded in the world around us. Strictly speaking, Chinese does not have an alphabet, but rather a vast collection of ideographs which, unlike western letters, *were* originally pictures of the natural world. Understandably, after 5000 years of evolution, most modern Chinese characters are hardly recognisable as representing some aspect of reality. However there are still some, like tree:

in which the similarity between sign and referent can be clearly seen.[12]

The east proved to be a gateway for me. It opened up a strange sequence of occurrences which cannot easily be described. Perhaps the English word "concatenation" comes closest: a long chain of linked events.

Divination

It all started one May evening. There was the first cold edge of winter in the air as I sat before my computer looking up the word "divide" in Chinese. By then Kate had insisted that I install satellite TV as she was feeling "terribly neglected in the evenings". Suffice to say the atmosphere in our home at that stage, notwithstanding the changing of the seasons, was generally chilly!

I had located a Chinese/English conversion website, which displayed the Chinese ideograph for the English word, with some background on how the ideograph originated. I had already looked up several words topical to my Quest ("why", "reason", "dilemma", and "twig") but had not encountered anything of great interest. Now it was "divide's" turn and I watched the

---

[12] Although Chinese has been criticised (mainly by westerners) as being a clumsy and unwieldy language, it is the only language on the planet that has survived for 5000 years.

computer screen intently. The ideographs that made up "divide" were obscure, including (amongst other things) a pictograph representing a knife. For a moment I thought that perhaps this had something to do with a "two-edged sword" but, as I searched further, I could find no other more meaningful link.

Disappointed, I was about to exit the site when, about four entries below "divide", the word "divine" caught my eye. That these words were in close proximity needn't have come as a surprise; after all, they both share all of the same letters but one.

The very first character making up the word "divine" was an unusual shape. It was only after examining it for a while that it dawned on me that it held a lot of similarity to the letter Y, only it was upside down.

My curiosity aroused, I clicked on the character to learn about its original roots. The hyperlink was a slow one and took several long seconds before arriving at the new page. Then there, flashing on the shimmering screen, were the words: "This Chinese character is very ancient and derives its shape from a forked twig. Such twigs were possibly used in divination rituals".

Divination! Here, at last, was a divine link to the Pythagorean letter.

It was only later, when the discovery had sunken in, that I realised that Y shaped twigs had possessed mystical properties all along. Had Y shaped twigs not been used by water diviners for centuries to locate underground water? I had read about these divining rods before in my life, but had never linked them to my Quest. For months now I had been searching for the seemingly supernatural properties contained in that forked twig fifteen years before, but during this entire period, the process of water divination had never once crossed my mind. But now, finally, I had *twigged!*

I have spent many days and nights since that breakthrough pondering at how such a seemingly blatant connection could have eluded me for so long. Quite simply, I had got hold of "*the wrong end of the stick*"! The Chinese word for "divine" was indeed upside down. But I had also been holding the wrong end of the stick in a deeper sense, for I had been approaching the branch in the professor's office as a letter all along, and not as the twig of wood which it really was. I had been committing one of the greatest mistakes we westerners commit unknowingly all of the time, and that is the mistake of *not seeing things as they really are*. Or, to use another well worn cliché, "*I couldn't see the wood for the trees*"!

Water divination (or "dowsing" as it is popularly known) is one of those practices that defy categorisation. The ability of certain "gifted" individuals to walk across a tract of land with nothing but a forked twig in hand, and accurately pinpoint underground water, is beyond the powers of scientific explanation. Despite exhaustive efforts to detect some measurable force field between the water and the twig, nothing rational has ever surfaced. Indeed, if it weren't that multinational companies pay huge amounts to dowsers to locate hidden water (and minerals and treasures), dowsing could well have been thrown onto the same "hocus pocus", arbitrary and random pile to which coincidences are relegated.

It was through a dictionary that I managed to come up with my own sort of explanation for divination. The dictionary definition of "divination" is "*to discover through intuition...*"[13] When I looked up the word "intuition" in turn, I found that, amongst other things, intuition ultimately meant "*without reason*". Here was the key. Had I not been looking for a way to proceed in my Quest that was *beyond the rational*? What better solution

[13] **The Concise Oxford Dictionary**

than to replace "intellect" with "intuition"? Instead of using the professor's branch as the question "*Why?*", I would now use the branch as a divining rod. Instead of being a symbol of the *division* in my life, it would become a symbol of the *divine* in my life.

As I reflected upon this, it dawned on me that I had already been using the Y as a divining rod for some time. When I was floundering, had I not said to myself, "*If I keep the Y central, and follow my enquiry where it takes me, I am sure I will find some pointers*"? Had this not been my intuition quietly at work? Was it not the divining rod that had pointed me to China? Intuition's ways are far more subtle and fleeting than the ways of the intellect, I was learning!

I am eternally awe-struck by the seemingly never-ending supply of secrets that a simple twig of wood can harbour. And this, the latest secret, was like discovering pure magic, because the divining rod had a divine element, *literally*. The spell *was* in the spelling. Millions of lives are devoted every day throughout the world to seeking some sign of the divine, and I, a mere financial advisor living in Durban, South Africa, had the sign in my very hand.

Pilgrimage

It was in this "spellbound" frame of mind that I pondered the next leg of my Quest. I arrived at the insight that my Quest had experienced enough "armchair travel". It now required some real travel. Since 1984 I had been lucky enough to travel fairly extensively throughout the world, but the one place to which I had never been was the east. I now felt an urgent calling to go there and, eager to honour my newfound "intuitional method", I took the calling seriously.

In the back of my mind there was another factor that fueled this calling. I had never forgotten about the mysterious woman who had appeared on my first day in Addington Hospital. Under her arm she had clutched a thick book on Chinese philosophy. Was this somehow linked to my current search?

I began to make travel enquiries. Once again intuition guided me. My first choice, China, proved to be a non-starter, because a little research revealed that, due to the stifling presence of the Communist bureaucracy, this land would not be conducive to spontaneous mystical research. Thailand and Nepal were considerations but I concluded that these countries had become too touristy and I wanted somewhere unspoiled, somewhere that retained the purity of its ancient heritage. When a travel agent mentioned Bhutan, something just clicked.

I had a month and a half's leave due to me and so, on a whim (really just another way of saying "through intuition"), I decided to take my pilgrimage to the Far East. I suppose in a way that is how all personal pilgrimages start out – in response to a voice that can only be heard within.

There was another, less lofty and more practical reason for my journey. My increasing preoccupation with my night-time activities had finally begun to impact on my business duties. My staff had picked up that there was "something going on", I sensed, and were starting to talk. I knew that one day in the very near future there was going to be an almighty either/or showdown between my Quest and my business! But anxious not to face this dilemma until I absolutely had to, I took leave.

Kate eventually got over her first objections. She went through a phase of wanting to come with me on the trip. But when I emphasised that I was going to "rough it" and it would be low budget all the way – no hotels, swimming pools or nightlife – she lost interest. Within three weeks I had arrived in the tiny city of Thimphu, capital of the mountain kingdom of Bhutan. Situated between Tibet and India, it is a remote country nestled in the heart of the Himalayan mountain range.

Intuition or no intuition, doubts about my choice surfaced within days of my arrival! Although Thimphu possessed a unique kind of beauty, with never-ending blue hills sprawling in every direction, it was also very backward and rundown. Privately I had hoped that I might run into an enlightened lama. But as I traipsed through the squalid streets, making my way through the throngs of poverty-stricken Bhutanese, I wondered if I was going to find anyone who could even understand English, let alone *explain* the secrets of his or her enlightenment for my illumination.

I spent many hours, in those first few days, hanging out at a quaint teahouse opposite the open-air vegetable market. A few westerners drifted in and out, mostly Australians and Canadians who were on one year teaching assignments. I made small talk with one or two of them but was painfully aware that these brief contacts were not going to point me in the right direction.

On the fourth day, with growing disappointment, I was walking down a side street taking in the rows of topsy-turvy shops, when I stumbled upon a clue. Most of the shops appeared to sell an identical array of vegetables, spices and blankets, and were adorned with signwriting scrawled in Bhutanese across the dusty windows. I was about to cross the street when an English sign in a tiny shop at the end of the street caught my attention. The sign said "Wisdom Shoppe", and what I presumed must have been the Bhutanese version of this (along with a few other language versions) was written below.

My curiosity aroused, I made my way to the intriguing looking shop. This end of the street was a little quieter than the rest and, besides the odd cat curled up in a pool of sunlight on the sidewalk, there was not much sign of life. In the distance the majestic snow capped peaks of the Himalayas gazed down on the city.

I peered through the windows into the dimly lit interior. The inner walls of the shop were lined on either side by rickety bamboo shelves and on these shelves was a strange assortment of articles: jars containing orange and brown powders; prayer mats; embroidered cushions; and peculiar amulets. There didn't seem to be anybody about, but a collection of books on one shelf caught my eye. One or two titles were in English and I pushed open the lilac painted door and went in.

Inside there was the subtlest hint of incense and once the door closed behind me the hubbub of the city completely disappeared. I became aware of a striking stillness, and remained motionless as I peered at the books. There was a rustle and I sensed that somebody had emerged from a doorway at the back. I turned and my eyes engaged with those of a Bhutanese woman. She must have been in her late fifties as her long, dark hair was streaked with grey, and she had deep laughter lines at the corners of her eyes. Otherwise, though, her skin was remarkably smooth with that soft, golden-brown sheen common to the Bhutanese people. More than anything else I was aware of her eyes, for they possessed a sort of lucidity I have seldom seen, a look that seemed to penetrate right through me.
"Can I be helping you?" she asked, in a very soft voice, which seemed incongruous with such piercing eyes.
"I was, um, just looking for a book on, um, Chinese divination." I enunciated the words slowly, so she would grasp them. She smiled, turned, and disappeared into the room at the back. A moment later she came out with a grimy looking book, which she placed on the counter in front of me. **I Ching**, it said on the cover.
"This book – Chinese classic on divination," she announced calmly. "English name is **Book of Changes**." I had heard of it before, and vaguely knew that it had something to do with fortune telling.

Coins *Coin*ciding
That night, in the dancing light of a butter lamp, I set about reading the **I Ching**. It is a book that is consulted as an oracle, by seekers of wisdom. Its origins are said to stretch back to the dawn of Chinese history from which it has been passed down

by countless generations of learned sages. Perhaps the most striking aspect of the **I Ching** (which seems to differentiate it from the millions of other books on the planet) is that it is an *interactive* book; it requires the reader's participation.

The **I Ching** is structured into 64 different hexagrams, each hexagram consisting of a unique combination of six individual lines (hence "hex" for six). Every hexagram represents a different state of change within the universe and each one has an attached passage of advice on how best to negotiate this change. Selecting which of the 64 hexagrams is appropriate to the reader's circumstances is where the interactivity comes in. The reader participates in the process by casting a series of coins while contemplating the problem at hand. The way in which the coins land (whether heads or tails), determines the structure of the hexagram and this unique hexagram becomes the "chosen" oracle.

The minute I read about this coin throwing process, my interest was aroused, for it appeared that the entire validity of the **I Ching** rested on the exact dichotomy I'd exposed in the first leg of my Quest: the dichotomy between *arbitrary* and *meaningful*. To our scientific western minds, the seemingly random tossing of coins could in no way be linked to an ancient text. If it so happened that the chosen text *did* appear relevant to the reader's circumstances, then this would surely be attributed to coincidence (merely coins *coin*ciding), and the whole thing would be deemed nonsensical quackery.

The Chinese, however, did believe that there was a meaningful link between reader and text. I found it particularly interesting when the author explained that this link could not be understood within the realm of reason, but rather through the process of *intuition*. The workings of the **I Ching** become quite obscure to the rational mind, he said, because just as the reader reads the **I Ching**, the **I Ching** (through the interaction of the coin-tossing) "reads the reader".

The Master Arrives Without Leaving

I was aware throughout my readings that I hadn't yet come across any Y shaped twigs. A second trip to the Wisdom Shoppe was called for. The next day, I wandered aimlessly around the vegetable market for a while before making my way back to the narrow side street. The shopkeeper smiled at me warmly the minute I walked into the shop. I approached the counter with a quickening heartbeat and she asked, “You like?”

I told her that it was interesting but asked her if, this time, she had anything on Chinese dowsing. I had concluded overnight that this might be a better approach to finding my Y shaped twig. “Ah yes!” she said in a cheerful voice, gesturing me to wait while she walked over to a row of bookcases and ran her fingers along the spines of the books. The Bhutanese are not known for their tallness but she was on the short side even by their standards. Despite this, she exuded a powerful presence as she glided between the shelves, and my eyes couldn’t help following her.

When she returned she slapped a green covered paperback on the counter which said: The **Tao te Ching**.
“This book on Chinese Dowism”, she announced. I wasn’t quite sure what “Dowism” meant, and was about to protest that I was actually looking for Dows*ing*, not Dow*ism*. However, I decided I was lucky to have got even that far. I left the shop a few minutes later with the **Tao te Ching** in my bag and 100 *ngultrum*[14] less in my wallet. As I stepped out the door the cold, noisy blast of Thimphu hit me again.

The **Tao te Ching** didn’t take me as long to finish as the **I Ching** – the entire work is only 5000 words long. It was written by the great Chinese sage, Lao Tze, in 500 BC and was supposedly completed in one night. I discovered at the outset how the Bhutanese shopkeeper had confused the book with dowsing. The **Tao te Ching** is essentially the “Bible” of the Chinese religion Taoism, and the author went to great lengths in the introduction

[14] Bhutanese currency

to explain how the word "Tao" is actually pronounced "Dow" (hence Taoism – Dowism).

The pun between dowsing and Taoism was one of those pivotal coincidences in my Quest, but at the time I didn't notice. I was too busy trying to fathom the book's numerous paradoxes. The language was very simple and concise and yet the paradoxes seemed profound.

The Master stays behind
That is why he is ahead

The Master arrives without leaving

The path forward seems to go back

Approach it and there is no beginning
Follow it and there is no end

The Tao follows only itself

All of these statements seemed impossible to me. Feeling somewhat exasperated, I might well have closed the little book permanently, had it not been for the English translation of Tao (which the author went to great lengths to elucidate). The Tao means many things to many people, but its commonest translation is undoubtedly "The Way" or "The Path". This was more in tune with what I was looking for. After all, hadn't the very sentence that had sparked off this whole Quest mentioned a path? "*The lesson is this: Your life tells you your **path** if you stop to look at the clues it has been throwing at you all of this time*". I skimmed through the pages of the **Tao te Ching** once more, before blowing out the butter lamp.

But the next day my path into eastern philosophy entered rocky ground. My problems arose when I ran into the Yin and Yang.

I had resumed reading the **I Ching** and was learning how all of the 64 hexagrams, when broken down, were composed of nothing other than Yin and Yang elements. Each of the six lines that make up a single hexagram is either a full line:

———

or a broken line:

— —

The full lines are known as Yang lines and the broken lines as Yin lines.

The Yin and Yang have become fairly well known in the west via their interlocked shape, which constitutes the symbol of Tao. The symbol's appealing symmetry has led to its status as a popular cultural motif, ever-present adorning surfboards, woven into logos and hanging around the necks of pimply teenagers.

Less well known is the profound wisdom that is said to be encapsulated by the timeless Tao. According to the ancient Chinese, far from being merely a "nice design", the Yin and Yang are the basic building blocks of the entire universe. The Yin (black) is commonly regarded as the "female" force and is representative of the dark, receptive womb of earth, while the Yang (white) is regarded as the "male" force and is representative of the penetrating light of the sunlit heavens. Many other descriptions are also used, such as "night and day", "winter and summer" and "yielding and dominant".

I guess it was the "night and day" description that triggered my discontent, because the more I mulled over it, the more obvious it seemed that here in front of me, in the tiny mountain capital of Thimphu, was the treacherous dualism I'd been so keen to escape. "Good and evil", "mind and matter", "white and black", "Yin and Yang" – wasn't it all the same? The ancient Chinese had simply called it another name. My subsequent reading confirmed my suspicions, for it was blatant that each line of the hexagram was confronted with a terrible dilemma; it had to be *either* Yin *or* Yang. There was no middle ground.

That evening, as I watched the sun sinking into the mauve sea of the Himalayas, I faced the possibility that my answers might not lie in Thimphu. If there was one thing that I did not wish to find in the east it was dualism and the failure to discover anything remotely similar to divining rods was beginning to annoy me. Perhaps I should have gone to India or Tibet? It wasn't too late to change my travel plans.

Let Go India

The next morning I got up early and set out to find a travel agent of some sort that could enlighten me on other destinations. But it soon became apparent that the Bhutanese did not travel much outside of Bhutan. I could not find any shop resembling a travel agency and the one airline office that I did find offered only "ticket sales", nothing else. I resolved that I would have to read up on India and Tibet myself. Not knowing of any other bookshops, I arrived back at the Wisdom Shoppe. But this time I couldn't go in, because the little shop was dark inside and across the front door was a sign that said, "DO NOT DISTURB. IN TUITION".

With nothing better to do, I made my way over to the teahouse by the market and ordered a jug of steaming green tea. With the exception of one table in the corner, where a young guy with blonde hair sat, the place was empty. I greeted him. I had seen him before at the teahouse. As I slowly sipped my tea I hoped that we might strike up a conversation, but it never materialised. Despite his usual hearty greeting in a loud English accent, the blonde guy always appeared to be immersed in his reading. I had caught a glimpse of the titles of the books and they seemed to be highly scientific and mathematical tomes.

After about forty minutes, I paid for the tea, nodded farewell to the Englishman, and retraced my footsteps to the Wisdom Shoppe. This time it was open and the shopkeeper was standing smiling in the exact same posture in which I had left her a few days before. The delicately incensed air greeted my nostrils. In the stillness of the small shop I suddenly became aware of the frustration that had built up inside of me over the last day or two. Evidently, the shopkeeper could also detect it, for her eyes seemed to radiate compassion.

"Do you have any travel books in stock?"
"Travel books? What kind of travel books is young man wanting?" she enquired.
"Anything on India or Tibet," I said. "Maybe a **Let's Go India**, or something."
She stood considering my words for a while and then shook her head slowly (almost with a touch of sadness, I thought). "No such books," she said.
I thanked her, turned around, and was about to leave the shop when, in that same calm, quiet voice she said, "My friend, you need 'Let Go India', not **Let's Go India**". She chuckled gently. The words were totally unexpected and I whirled around to face her again: "What do you mean?"
"You hold onto things too tight," she said. "You need to let go."
I explained to her that there was something that I was looking for, and only when I found it would I be able to let go. "India not going to be helping you," she said. "Nowhere in Asia going to be helping you."
"Why not?"
She smiled compassionately at that, and said in a quiet, almost resigned voice, "Wherever you go – there you are". "You don't understand," I said. "What I am looking for is not in Thimphu."
She didn't answer me immediately, but just stood pondering, letting the silence build up around us. It was only when I was feeling positively uncomfortable amidst the soundlessness, that

she asked, "What is it that young friend seeks?" I warmed to this and explained to her that I was looking for anything to do with the forked shaped twigs that the Chinese used in divination rituals. I took a pen from my pocket and drew the Y shape on a scrap of paper, to show her what I meant. She examined the paper briefly and then announced humbly, "If friend can't find Y shape in Yin and Yang, friend can't find Y shape anywhere".

Those were the words that echoed around my head as I strode back to the guesthouse that Wednesday morning in Thimphu. Both the Yin and the Yang *did* commence with a Y! There was, after all, some middle ground between these opposing elements. Was it once again "mere" coincidence, or a sign that I was on the right path? My previous experiences all pointed to the latter. That night I resolved to find out more about what kind of tuition the Wisdom Shoppe conducted.

The next day I was up fresh and early and after a hurried bowl of steaming oats, I set out to the shop. I found the shopkeeper waiting in her usual spot and announced that I wished to find out more about the tuition that she had conducted the day before. At first she seemed to feign ignorance. When I pointed out the "Do Not Disturb" sign, a seriousness appeared to come over her.
"Young friend not ready to learn."
"Why not?" I protested.
"Young friend is having problems letting go."
Her reference once again to the "Let Go" issue irked me. This woman spoke in the same indecipherable riddles as the **Tao te Ching**, I thought to myself.

She obviously detected my disappointment for she beckoned for me to follow as she made her way through the tiny doorway at the back. I followed her, stooping to avoid the arch. I blinked as I stepped into the interior – it was slightly dimmer than the first room. It was also considerably larger and I wondered why the

COSMIC
YO YO

shopkeeper kept all her merchandise crammed in the front when she had so much space inside. Besides a small candle burning steadily in one corner, and a large square black cushion in the middle of the wooden floor, the room was empty. The walls were white and bare except for another door at the rear.

"Sit down," she said, gesturing at the black cushion, "I fetch tea".

She disappeared through the doorway at the back. I became aware of an even more powerful silence as I sat on the black cushion in the middle of the room. It was one of those silences that rings loudly in your ears despite there being no source of the ringing; it reminded me of the sound of the sea that you can hear when you put a seashell to your ear.

Before long, she reappeared with a small tray of tea in one hand, and another black cushion under her arm. She sat down cross-legged on the cushion opposite me, gestured at my teacup and said, "You like?"
I nodded and she started to pour tea into my cup. I watched the olive liquid slowly rising to the rim, and then reaching the rim and then overflowing the rim so that a puddle of tea started to spread on the tray. "That's enough!" I cried, "That's enough!" in an alarmed tone. She didn't seem to hear me though; she just continued pouring and the puddle grew bigger. Then, in that gentle, soothing voice of hers she said, "You see, my friend, just like the tea cup, you cannot hold anything new inside your head because it is already too full".

She stopped pouring my tea. She went on to tell me that the only way I would learn anything new was if I emptied some of the clutter, and the only way to do that was through meditation, not through more books. "Many people are thinking they can buy wisdom at Wisdom Shoppe," she said, "but true wisdom is not being for sale. If young friend really wants to find truth, young friend must come to observe meditation early tomorrow morning".

Seeing Things Exactly as They Are

I got up before the sun and was at Sam's shop at our agreed time of 6.30am. "My name to you is Sam," she had said the day before, and when I had asked her if I could bring anything such as a pen and paper along, she had replied sternly "Bring nothing – *especially not a pen*!"

Wrapped in a flowing maroon robe, Sam greeted me with her usual quiet warmth. She hung up the "Do Not Disturb. In Tuition" sign, and I followed her into the inner room. She sat me down cross-legged on the cushion, with my hands lying lightly in my lap and my shoulders relaxed but my spine straight.

For the next twenty minutes she proceeded to give me basic instruction in the practice of meditation. It seemed simple enough: I was to sit very still, very quietly, very relaxed and *let go* of everything in the world. All I was to think about was my breathing, one breath at a time: the in-breath, the pause, and then the out-breath; then the pause, and then the in-breath again. If any other thoughts came to my mind, I shouldn't grasp at them, she said, but should gently let them go in the same manner that I let go the out-breath. We were to start the first week with daily sessions of twenty-five minutes and then gradually build up to hour-long sessions.

Apart from aching shoulders, the first session went really well. When Sam struck her little gong indicating the end of the session I told her that I had found it relatively easy. In response she smiled at me, in that compassionate sort of manner to which I was becoming accustomed. It was only during our session on about the third day that I suddenly realised that, without my being aware of it, my mind had been full of thoughts for nearly every minute of meditation right from the beginning. It was true that when I had started out each time I had concentrated on my breathing. But then somewhere along the line, I had unconsciously slipped into everyday thoughts. They hadn't been extraordinary thoughts, just thoughts about home, about Kate, about Sam and about the **I Ching**. But I had been *thinking* – and the main point of meditation, I'd learned thus far, was *not* to think!

This sudden realisation startled me, not so much because of the fact that I had not yet mastered meditation, but rather because I had spent over an hour in the last three days sitting in thought *without being aware* that I was sitting in thought! It was this complete lack of awareness that alarmed me, for it exposed very clearly a blind spot in my own mind.

At the end of that meditation session I told Sam about my "failure". To my surprise she appeared to be delighted! I spent the rest of that day trying to comprehend the reason for her apparent approval. It was only two sessions later that she explained why she had been happy: "Before that day, Christopher was unaware that he was not meditating. Now Christopher is aware that he is not meditating. Meditation is about awareness. Awareness that you are not meditating is first step towards meditating". Once again, her answer had had that distinctly paradoxical ring to it.

She went on in subsequent sessions to tell me that the problem that I had identified of not being aware of what was going on in my own mind was the problem for all of humankind, although very few people know they have this problem. At least I had caught a glimpse of the problem, she said. Our daytime thoughts are like our night-time dreams – we are not completely awake while we are thinking them. Meditation, she explained, was about becoming awake. As to the problem of how to get rid of the thoughts once you'd realised you were thinking them, her advice was, "Let go".

Actually, "letting go", I was to discover, was the easy part. Becoming aware that you were thinking at all was the hard part. Once you became aware, the thoughts almost dissipated of their own accord, and you could return to experiencing your breathing. But then, like a thief in the night, another thought would carry you away, and sometimes ten full minutes could slip by before you realised that your breathing experience had been hi-jacked. Nevertheless, despite a perpetually sore back, I persevered with my meditation, determined to catch the thief of thought as early as I could. Sometimes I felt like I was making a little progress, other times not.

I had started doing two meditation sessions a day by that stage and Sam seemed happy enough with my progress. She was ever ready with her paradoxical answers. One day, when I complained, "I'm struggling with my meditation," she replied swiftly, "That is why".
"What do you mean?" I asked.
"That is why – because you are struggling."
She explained to me, "One must not struggle and fight; one must be gentle, kind and patient with oneself".
Another time, when I moaned, "My meditation is getting nowhere," she chuckled to herself, and quipped, "If only you were so lucky – nowhere is the right place for your meditation to go".

During those first few weeks Sam assured me that the outcome of proper meditation would be the attainment of a state of awakened consciousness wherein "*you can see things exactly as they are*". But when I pressed her to describe what this state was like, she told me that words couldn't describe it. "It must be *experienced*," she explained earnestly. Trying to describe it, she'd said, would be like trying to describe the colour red to a blind man. "No matter what nice words you were using, he would not be knowing the colour red until the day his sense of sight was awakened".

I often marvel at that description. On more than one occasion I've set out to disprove her theory and write a letter to a blind person describing a colour. But if you don't believe how impossible it is, just try it. It would seem that some things really are beyond the grasp of words.

It wasn't only the hope of attaining an awakened state that kept me persevering with meditation. In between sessions I had not completely abandoned my journeys into the Chinese classics. It finally seemed as if I was making a little progress. It's true that Sam gave me some cryptic pointers along the way, but I was sure that there was something more than that – almost as if the texts had become more lucid since my meditation had begun. Whether this was so or not, I will never know for sure, as anybody who knows anything about meditation will confirm that it takes years and years of devoted practice for significant changes in perception to occur. Nevertheless, some of the things that I was encountering in the books were beginning to make more sense in relation to findings from earlier on in my Quest.

The Roots Below

One of the more helpful doors that had opened up was the door of Carl Jung. Jung had started out as a close friend of Sigmund Freud, the renowned "discoverer" of the Unconscious. Freud challenged the rational worldview by claiming that below the rational mind there lurked a whole "other" mind – the unconscious – and this mind was everything but rational. Its agenda was far more sinister.

On the day that I was contemplating Freud's concept of the unconscious an important thing happened. Sam asked, with a mischievous grin, if I had managed to "grasp non-grasping yet". I replied that I didn't understand, to which she replied, "While you *stand under* the tree looking only at the branches – you will never *understand* the tree".

This statement took me by surprise, for it was the first time that Sam had made any reference to trees or branches. Had she perhaps

THE ROUTES ABOVE
& THE ROOTS BELOW

taken my earlier reference to Y shaped twigs more seriously than I had given her credit for? (I was to be surprised like this on many occasions during my stay in Bhutan; for often I would say the most fleeting thing to Sam, positive that she hadn't picked up on it, but nothing ever escaped her.)

That evening I contemplated the implications of Sam's unexpected statement. What did she mean by looking "only at the branches" of the tree? Gradually I realised that, up until then, there was a very important part of trees that I'd overlooked (literally). Trees (with their trunks and branches) had long since been a symbolic part of my Quest, and yet up to that point I had never considered that below the ground was a whole other side of trees: the roots. If you really want to understand a tree you have to consider its roots, buried out of sight in the dark reaches of the earth. In other words; there is *more to the tree than meets the eye.*

And that is where the unconscious comes in. For with this new holistic picture of the tree in my mind, some important connections between the roots and the unconscious emerged. Were Freud and Jung not saying that the branches of the behaviour that could be scientifically observed and measured above the soil were only one side of the story? Was the implication not that, at sub-ground level, there was a whole "other" world: the invisible world of underground roots (the unconscious) that had just as much, if not greater, effect on the tree?

Freud believed that the roots of the unconscious were driven by sexual desires.[15] It was this obsession with sex that ultimately led to his and Jung's divergence. Jung agreed wholeheartedly that underlying the rational mind was a vast and unexplored unconscious mind, but he saw the great need in humans as being for primordial spiritual meaning rather than sex. Jung recognised that, just as the conscious mind was governed by rationality, the

---

[15] Had Freud examined my Quest he might well have said that the whole thing had to do with the Y chromosome of my male-hood; that I had an almighty phallic fixation and that, subconsciously, the Y actually represented a giant penis for me. He would probably have proceeded to explain that the penis was the ultimate "connector" that I was looking for – the living divining rod that dipped and rose as it got closer to its treasure.

unconscious mind was governed by a different, irrational force that he often referred to as *intuition*.

And that is exactly how Jung landed up in this ancient Chinese text which I was reading each night in Thimphu. So intrigued had Jung been with the intuitive power of coincidences, that he had written the introduction to the version of the **I Ching** that I now held in my hands. He too had recognised the mysterious enchantment contained within the coinciding of coins.

It was heartening to me that so respected a western thinker had devoted so much time to the study of coincidences. Jung even went so far as to coin a new term for coincidences – "synchronicity" – a core concept within his later theories. What is important to point out about synchronicity is that it attaches a critical adjective to coincidences. Jung's coincidences are "*meaningful* coincidences". Had I at last found an acclaimed western psychologist who, despite his scientific approach, challenged the conventional "random and arbitrary" explanation offered in response to coincidences and the like?

Jung was specifically interested in the Chinese belief that the **I Ching** and the reader *were* connected, that there *was* a meaningful link between the two, that the reader's selection process of the appropriate hexagram was not one of random coincidence but of *meaningful* coincidence. He was intrigued by the psychological aspect of this process, wherein the *internal* world of the reader interacted with the *external* world of the text. Jung described this interaction best in his own words (from the Introduction to the **I Ching**):[16]

> *...Synchronicity takes the coincidence of events in time and space as meaning something more than mere chance, namely, a peculiar interdependence of objective events with the subjective (psychic) states of the observer.*

---

[16] The Richard Wilhelm translation.

When I first read these words, my heart leapt with excitement! Suddenly, my whole journey to the east was beginning to help me make sense of my Ward 24 experiences. It is difficult to express in words all the connections that were to become clear as a result of this new way of thinking…

Inner Worlds and Outer Worlds

Perhaps a good launching point would be to start with a description Sam gave me of the Yin and the Yang. Her explication was very enriching.

"If young friend wants to truly understand Yin and Yang, young friend must observe breathing during meditation very carefully. In-breath is Yin and out-breath is Yang."

This description appealed to me immediately because the cyclic nature of breathing seemed to capture – far more accurately than "male and female" or "heaven and earth" – the cyclic nature of the Yin/Yang symbol. Integral to the Yin/Yang interplay is the concept of reversal, best described by the Chinese proverb, "*If you take something to its extreme – it becomes its opposite*". This principle is ingeniously illustrated by the little dots of opposing colour contained in each of the Yin and Yang. For they are "seeds" and it is exactly at the point that the Yin and Yang are at their fullest, that the seed for the other is born. This "reversal" principle reverberates in the breath too, because it is only when the out-breath is at its fullest, that the in-breath can commence, and the in-breath at its fullest, that the out-breath can commence. There is an interdependence between Yin and Yang rather than a dualistic opposition. Without the one, you cannot have the other. Exclusion is an impossibility. Either/or is not an option!

Perhaps of even greater relevance was the notion of "outer" and "inner" implied by the breath. It is ultimately this distinction, more than any other, that underlies all of the dualism I had hitherto come across in my Quest. Had Descartes not commenced by identifying an *external* material world, which was subject to doubt, and an *internal* non-material world which he could not doubt? Besides mind and matter, was there not another split, along an even deeper fault line: between the *inner* world and the *outer* world, between "subjective" and "objective"? Jung's "*objective events*" and "*subjective states of the observer*"?

The outer/inner distinction can be seen embedded in the traditional descriptions of the Yin and Yang too. For the "womb of the earth" (Yin) and the "abounding heavens" (Yang) are strongly segregated into outer and inner paradigms. Male and female can also be differentiated along these lines with the male genitals external in nature and the female's internal. And surely the conscious and the unconscious mind could be analogised as the outer and the inner mind?

The analogy that interested me most, from an inner/outer perspective, was the analogy of the symbolic tree. For are the branches of a tree not the external aspect that can be seen protruding into the bright heavens, while the roots are the internal aspect that inhabit the dark interior of the earth? Are the branches not the Yang side of the tree and the roots the Yin? And just like the in- and out-breath, are the branches and roots not *inter*dependent?

If you look at the roots of a tree they are not unlike the branches. These "internal branches" also fork out in symmetrical Y shapes. Just as the twig of the tree is the external Y, the root of the tree is the internal Y. And just as the external divining rod had been pointing outside of me for so long, the other was pointing within. Had the branch in the professor's office not been the outer material aspect of something that was inextricably rooted deep within me?

Coinciding with this new view of the professor's branch, I recalled something strangely familiar. On the night of my vision, when

I had seemed to leave the car and look back down on myself lying on the back seat, I had seen two selves, a black self and a white self, lying *head to toe* with each other. This "head to toe" aspect had never before seemed significant. But weren't the Yin and Yang also positioned "head to toe" with each other, the black one on one side, and the white one on the other?

Symbolism, says Jung, is the language of the unconscious. Shapes and patterns contain deep metaphorical meaning. Symbolism was the medium in which I experienced things in 1984, once my unconscious Yin self had been awakened.

But maybe there was still unresolved unconscious conflict. For, what are the letters of our alphabets other than symbols? In fact, are they not the most universal of human symbols? Why my ongoing obsession with them? And what about my nightmare of the forked branch? Dreams are also a language of the unconscious. Was the nightmare not a personal wake-up call from my unconscious, a cry for help?

Being a medical psychologist, Jung's ultimate concern with the human mind was what happens when it gets sick. The interaction of the conscious and unconscious mind was at the very crux of mental illness, he said, for mental illness is the direct manifestation of these two minds being out of "synch"(synchronicity?). In addition to an individual "unconscious", Jung firmly believed that there existed a "group unconscious" which he called the "collective unconscious". Through this collective unconscious the group mind directly affects the individual mind.[17]

It was this observation of the collective unconscious that helped Jung predict the World Wars of his lifetime. With the relentless march of science and rationalism that preceded the wars, Jung was concerned that the group conscious mind, which was predominantly intellectual, was gaining an unhealthy dominance

---

[17] This phenomenon has gained credibility since observation of the simultaneous "outbreak" of newly acquired behaviour traits displayed by monkeys inhabiting neighbouring islands. Clearly the new behaviour could not have been communicated over the water so there must have been some other, "telepathic" link.

over the group unconscious mind, which was predominantly intuitional. He argued that this repression of the unconscious was leading humans to "lose touch" with themselves, and he prophesied that the internal conflict would soon manifest into large-scale external conflict in Europe.

It was his search for an alternative to Europe's preoccupation with science and "progress" that led Jung to Asia and the **I Ching**. In the oriental mind he found a much healthier balance between intellect and intuition. Here were a people who respected the harmony between the inner and outer states making up the universe.

A Spanish Sailor

At the time that I made all these "theoretical" discoveries, I wasn't sure if Sam had any knowledge of the academic theory underlying eastern philosophy. I knew that she was intelligent. But she always seemed to scorn books and the notion of finding wisdom in their pages. Wisdom was, for her, a *practice*, a participatory process, not a passive "armchair" one. Wisdom was a way of life and could not be captured by the pattern of some cleverly selected black letters decorating small rectangles of white paper. And yet, notwithstanding her anti-scholarly stance, Sam always astounded me with her ability to come up with answers to the most complicated of theoretical problems. It was to her that I turned when I found things that I simply could not comprehend.

Despite the great strides forward that I had made in the Chinese classics, there still existed one set of paradoxes that I couldn't solve. They were what I had begun to think of as "the terrible paradoxes" contained in the **Tao te Ching**:

> *The Master stays behind*
> *That is why he is ahead*

The Master arrives without leaving

The path forward seems to go back

Approach it and there is no beginning
Follow it and there is no end

The Tao follows only itself.

For the life of me I couldn't work any sense into these statements, so I took them one day, written on a piece of paper, to Sam. She laughed out loud the minute she read them. Realising that she had offended me, she reassured me that I was "too clever" to understand these statements. This did nothing to quell my doubts. For some time I had suspected that intelligence and intuition might work in opposite directions; maybe having a high IQ obstructs your intuition rather than enhancing it?

After our second meditation that day, I brought up the paradoxes again but her responding comments were every bit as paradoxical as the statements themselves. "Young friend is belonging to Flat Earth Society," she said. And then, as I was about to leave she chuckled, "Only loopy people are understanding true Tao. Only people who are around the bend". As hard as I tried, I couldn't make sense of her utterances.

It was only about two days later, after a particularly long meditation session, that she asked me, "Young friend, are you still wondering how the Tao follows only itself?"
"Yes!" I replied. How could anything ever follow itself? "Young friend must observe carefully," she said, holding up a piece of red silk with the Yin and Yang delicately embroidered onto its face.
"What does young friend see?"
I told her that I saw the Yin and the Yang. "And what are Yin and Yang doing?" she asked. I pondered, for I had always thought

of the Yin and Yang as a static pattern, devoid of any "doings". She waited, motionless, as I sat cross-legged on the black cushion staring at the piece of silk.

Slowly, slowly it came to me.

The Yin and Yang were moving in a circle. That was it – a circle! I felt like I heard a great gong go off in my head, for I knew, instantaneously, that only a circle could follow itself. And of what, other than a circle, could it be said, *"Approach it and there is no beginning, Follow it and there is no end"?*

That evening I was in high spirits. I knew intuitively that I had finally found my Way. The reason it had taken so long is the reason it takes all westerners so long. We are living in a totally different paradigm to the ancient Chinese – a *linear* world. Our sacred book, the Holy Bible, commences with the words, "*In the beginning...*" That is the way we have been brought up – in a space and time where everything has a beginning and an end. Our cognition is founded on Euclidean geometry and we picture the number system as a straight line that stretches to negative infinity on the one side and positive infinity on the other, with zero straddled helplessly like a "piggy in the middle".

This conception of things has always led enquiring minds into the most complex and apparently unsolvable of problems. For if we dare ask, "But what came before the beginning?" we are faced with an unbridgeable chasm. And what about the "chicken and egg" problem? Follow enough chickens and eggs back in time, and you are faced with the absurd question, "Which came first?"

These days most people in the west don't burden themselves for too long with these questions, concentrating rather on the more important tasks of working and consuming! The religious amongst us, who do wonder about these things, neatly place a wonderful

THE BEGINNING OF THE END THE BEGINNING OF THE END

THE BEGINNING OF THE END THE BEGINNING OF THE END

THE BEGINNING OF THE END THE BEGINNING OF THE END

©

MAKING ENDS MEET

"entity" just before the great chasm. This entity is God, and he has the handy ability to make all of the questions disappear! And where some posit God, the scientific place their little horizontal symbol of eight, which (although on an equally mystical footing to God) is apparently perfectly acceptable, mathematically.

But once you have grasped the Way (as I thought I had) all questions are answered. For it is simply a matter of Way – the way in which we look at things. It is the unnatural straight-line paradigm that causes so many of our problems. There are no straight lines in nature. But there are circles everywhere: the sun, the moon and earth; and even the *way* in which the earth moves around the sun. The natural way is the way of the circle.

It was Sam's statement about the Flat Earth Society that seemed to me best to illustrate the two worldviews of "linear" and "circular". The original view held by humankind was that the earth we live on is flat. Our great ancestors believed this. This "flat earth" is the linear view of the universe. This "flat earth" paradigm was the one that led to great monsters and sea dragons being depicted at the edge of the sea charts during the Dark Ages. And if you sailed too far, you were liable to drop off the edge of the world and be devoured.

Then one day an adventurous Spaniard, suspicious of the "flat earth" view, left a port in Spain in a sailing ship. He set sail in an easterly direction and vowed to carry on sailing eastward for as long as he could. He passed many strange lands. Eventually, after many months, a coastline – strangely familiar – loomed up on the eastern horizon. He recognised that this coastline was in fact the same Spanish coastline he had left so many months previously. A revelation!

Within a day or two thereafter the ship was back in its original port. The sailor had "proved" the "round earth" view and precipitated probably the greatest paradigm shift that has ever occurred to humankind.

WHY

WHY

WAY

WAY

©

FINDING THE WAY

If we take the Taoist viewpoint as the "round earth" view, suddenly all the paradoxes contained in the statements of the **Tao te Ching** disappear. Imagine, for a moment, that on the day that our Spanish sailor left his port in Spain, his Master had remained at the docks. Imagine the scene now, when the sailor catches sight of his port for the first time after circumnavigating the globe. As he enters the port he spies his Master who is at the dock to greet him. How easily could the sailor have said to his crew:

The Master stayed behind
That is why he is ahead.

And how perfectly sensible would it have been, on arriving at the dockside, to have said:

The Master arrives without leaving.

That night, while explaining his incredible journey to the astonished "flat earthers", how logical an observation would it have been to say:

The path forward seems to go back.

In this circular paradigm, we no longer have the problem of "what was before the beginning?" Before every egg comes a chicken, and before every chicken comes an egg. Nor, fifteen years previously, would I have had the problem of joining the Alpha and the Omega. They would never have been apart in the first place.

Absolutely

Unfortunately, shifting to this circular paradigm is no easy feat. The straight, steel railway line that runs within our western psyche is so deeply laid that it is near impossible to depart from. And if we do manage to leave, we are very quickly accused of "going off the rails". Great effort is made to get us "back on track", back onto the "straight and narrow". Sam had been right. Those who do manage to comprehend the Way are usually described as having gone "loopy" or worse, "around the bend".

Inherent in the eastern circular way of looking at things is a holism in which division and dichotomies dissolve. On a flat earth you could be sure that if you travelled in an easterly direction, you would always be travelling towards east. This unchanging quality of the flat earth east gives east a very important property – it is *absolute*. Absolute is a word that we English speakers like to throw about a lot, so it is important at this point to define in exactly what context I am going to use it. The definition I like best is, "*not relative or comparative…self-existent and conceivable without relation to other things*".[18]

On a round earth, though, things are not so straightforward. Living on the southern tip of Africa as I do, everything fits nicely into place. If I cross the Atlantic Ocean in a westerly direction I arrive in the land of the Wild West and if I cross the Indian Ocean in an easterly direction I get to the lands of the Far East. Fortunately for my worldview, the Cape of Good Hope[19] was the original halfway point for ships sailing from Western Europe to the east, and it was these sailors who drafted the original world maps (with America in the west and China in the east).

But what about the Hawaiians? If they fly due east they land up in the Wild West and by flying west they land up in the Far East! Clearly this "round world east" is not absolute, but rather, like the Yin or the Yang, *if it is taken to its extreme, it becomes its opposite*. In other words, far from being "*conceivable without relation to other things*", east in the round earth paradigm is completely dependent on its relation to other things. It all depends on your *point of view*. You have to look at the big picture, the whole, before deciding where east is to be found. In short, east is *relative* as opposed to absolute.

---

[18] **The Concise Oxford Dictionary**

[19] The reason that the Cape was originally named "The Cape of Good Hope" was because it was seen as a "*gateway to the riches of the east*".

This *relative* nature of the Way contained the answers I had been seeking. A world that is related is a world that is linked. In a relative world you cannot separate the "observer" and the "observed". "Observer" and "observed" are just the subjective and objective aspects of the same thing. All is connected: in-breath and out-breath; the **I Ching** and the reader; scientist and artist; word and world; root and twig. The true nature of "holism" can never be appreciated in the absolute world: there will always be Us's and Them's. There will always be discrimination and segregation. In the circular world, on the other hand, we are all *relatives* of the same family.

Unsurprisingly, the first theories of a round earth were greeted by the Church with great alarm. People who instigated these evil rumours were liable to be burned at the stake. Both the Islamic and the Judeo-Christian faiths, I would argue, are structured on absolutes. An absolute beginning, an absolute end, absolute good and absolute evil. The Tree of Knowledge of good and evil was merely the Tree of Knowledge of absolutes. It's not surprising that the cardinals of the early Church were so opposed to the concept of a round earth. If the *cardinal* points of the compass were to be challenged, how long would it be before their own absolute authority was threatened?

More worrying in terms of our modern society is that absolutes are the breeding ground of fundamentalism. Fundamentalists are convinced that if they continue travelling in an absolute direction they will eventually get to heaven. They are obsessed with the text, and blind to the con*text*. They cannot see that if they set out in one direction in order to distance themselves from the other direction, their extremism will land them back in the very place from which they were trying to escape. The context might be shrieking out to them that they are back in evil territory, but as long as their text says, "Go east", they stick to their guns. No such problems exist for the Taoist sages, as further verses that I gleaned from the **Tao te Ching** confirmed:

~~CON~~text©

FUNDAMENTALISM

Long and short define each other
Difficult and Easy support each other
High and low depend on each other

When people see some things as good
other things become bad.

In the Tao of life it is always the out-breath that defines the in-breath, and the in-breath that defines the out-breath. Yin and Yang are complementary, twins, and it is only their union that makes the perfect circle. Which is Yin and which is Yang is irrelevant. Indeed, if taken to its extreme, Yin can become Yang, and Yang, Yin. There is no absolute, indestructible Yin and no absolute, indestructible Yang. Life is dynamic and changeable, not static and absolute.

John

It is at this point that I need to bring in the young blonde Englishman I'd seen at the teashop. In between the Wisdom Shoppe meditation sessions I often frequented the teashop and had finally managed to strike up a conversation with him.

It turned out that he was on a one-year contract to teach maths and science at a high school near Thimphu. He had completed his doctorate in maths at Cambridge the previous year, and had come to Bhutan for a break from his studies. John was his name.

One day, shortly after discovering the Way, I was sipping green tea with John in the teahouse, when the conversation turned to what I was doing in Thimphu.
"I'm attempting to learn first hand about eastern philosophy and how it can help us westerners." I paused.
"Well? Learnt anything interesting yet?"
"The biggest thing I seem to have learnt so far is that easterners have a far more relative view of the world. It's almost as if we westerners are still stuck in absolute modes, if you know what

I mean."

"That is not true!" John immediately protested and proceeded to tell me about Einstein's theory of Relativity. The gist of Einstein's theory was that it apparently "proved" that the flow of time was not always unchangeable and *absolute* as had always been believed. Rather, the observer's position and speed in the universe had an effect on the measurement, so that time, in fact, was always *relative* to the observer.

John then got into some very technical areas of modern physics. Einstein even had a theory that Space and Time were both, contrary to the prevailing belief, curved rather than linear. I began to get excited. Here was some very respected hard science confirming the views of Sam and the Taoists.

But that wasn't the end of it. John explained that while Einstein's theories dealt with the universe on a grand scale, a quantum physicist, Werner Heisenberg, was examining matter at the other end of the spectrum (at the smallest scale). In 1925 he discovered that a type of Relativity affected the smallest particles in the universe too. One could never find out both the position and the velocity of an electron at the same time. This was because *the very act of measuring the electron had an effect on it.* In other words, like Einstein's stars and galaxies, particles could never be viewed *objectively*. The viewer (subject) will always have an effect on the viewed (object). It is not possible for us to take ourselves out of the system and view something within the system objectively because *we are part of the system*. The division of subjects and objects is false; we are all connected.

I Look Inside Myself and See

I was astounded at John's revelations. After all, how different was the concept of an **I Ching** reader having an influence on the I **Ching**, from the concept of an observer of quantum particles having an influence on the particles? Was the **I Ching** not ultimately composed of the same quantum particles? Maybe I had been wrong about science and the western way. Maybe scientists were more enlightened than I had thought.

But before I was able to overhaul my "thesis", John went on to say that, despite the recent changes in our scientific understanding of the universe, there were still problems. The "non-relative" worldview, which has been entrenched in the western frame of mind since the days of Newton, hadn't caught up with the leading scientists. He agreed with me that the traditional westerner still looked out at the world through a lens with a dated prescription. And this, according to John, was why we had so many environmental problems and the like in the modern world.

But what was to amaze me most, I only became aware of a day or two later. Slowly it dawned on me that despite the ancient Taoist's explanation of the universe being in precise concordance with that of modern science, there was no way that the Taoists could have arrived at their theories through *scientific* investigation. In 500 BC it was not known that the earth was round. And Einstein's theory of relativity was still light years away!

So, if the ancient sages hadn't used the scientific method, if they hadn't circumnavigated the globe in their Spanish galleons, how then *had* they predicted the nature of the universe so accurately? The answer to this question sounds absurd at first, but with the lack of an alternative it is the only answer that stands. The ancient Chinese achieved their accurate description of the universe through *intuition* – through *seeing things as they actually are.*

Just as the west attains its knowledge through studying the branches of the tree of life, the east attains its knowledge through observing the roots of the tree of life. Just as the west's investigations go *wandering externally*, the east's investigations go *wondering internally*. And both the branches of the tree, and the roots of the tree, share the same blueprints. The shape of the divining rod is present in both the twigs and the roots.

It is no wonder that eastern philosophy is often referred to as "mysticism". In our modern times, mysticism seems to be veiled in a sort of "hocus pocus" shroud, but if you go back to the dictionary, you find that a mystic is simply "*one who seeks through contemplation*". In the days that followed I was to find references to this "looking within" throughout the **Tao te Ching**:

The Master observes the world
But trusts his inner vision

Without looking out your window
You can see the essence of the Tao

How do I know this is true?
I look inside myself and see.

Strangely enough, Sam was not a devout Taoist. It is true that most of the texts she gave me were Taoist. But on the Wisdom Shoppe's shelves, alongside the **Tao te Ching** and the **I Ching**, were many books from other schools: Buddhism, Zen, Hinduism, even Confucianism. When I once pressed her for a definition of what she believed in she simply said, "There are many paths but only one road".
Another time when I asked her directly if she followed Taoism she replied quietly, "I am not believing in 'isms'. 'Isms' are leading to schisms".

The one thing that Sam did believe in was meditation – according to her, the true path to enlightenment. Meditation was looking within and *seeing things as they actually are.* Meditation was about dissolving the illusion of separateness in the universe. Enlightenment was achieved when the division of "self" and "other" disappeared – when, as Sam said one day: "*There is meditation but no meditator*".

Meditation without a meditator; a difficult concept to grasp. Over the months I've managed to attain an inkling of how this is meant

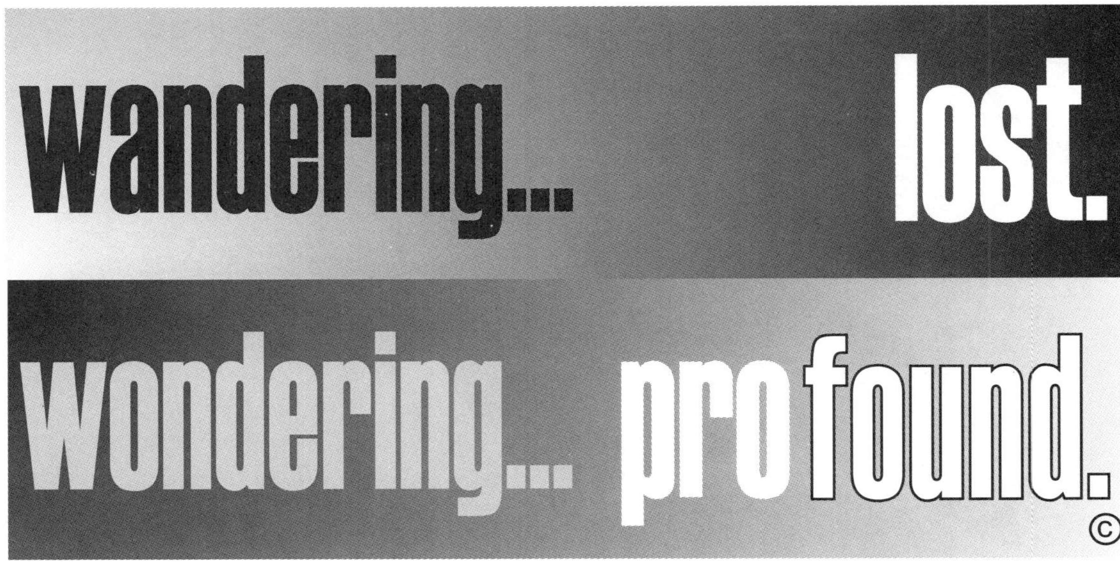

LOST AND FOUND

my stick
my stick
my stick
my stick
my stick
mystic
mystic
mystic
mystic
mystic
mystic
mystic
mystic
©

to work. Watch a highly accomplished dancer. There are moments when you could quite feasibly say that there seemed to be a dance but no dancer; the dancer and the dance have become one. Conversely, if you watch a poor dancer, there almost seems to be an awkward separateness that comes between the dancer and the dance. Dancing instructors often talk about "analysis paralysis", the phenomenon that affects beginner dancers when they over-analyse what they are doing instead of just doing it.

One day when I was sitting down on Sam's black cushion to meditate, I inadvertently let a sheet of Prozac pills slide out of my pocket. They landed on the floor and Sam spotted them immediately.
"What are pills for?" she asked suspiciously.
I was caught off guard but tried to evade her accusing eyes as best I could. "They're, um, to help me sleep at night… A doctor in South Africa gave them to me."
"Young friend needs meditation not medication! If you carry on with meditation carefully every day, soon you can throw pills out."

Medication versus meditation. Like divide and divine, only one letter differentiates the words. Yet their approaches are so different. The medication approach believes the answers lie on the outside, in chemicals contained in little pills, while the meditation approach believes that the answers lie within, and just need to be correctly accessed. I often wonder what Sam would have said to the psychiatrists who had pumped me full of medication in 1984. They believed they were curing my psychotic delusions. Sam would probably have prescribed meditation for them to help cure their absolute illusions.

Do Not Disturb
Perhaps the most difficult aspect of meditation is that it is one of the few "activities" (for want of a better word) that is one hundred percent personal in nature. Nobody, not even the most

skilled of meditation teachers, can feel or see what your personal meditation experience is like. Nobody can get inside of you and point you in the right direction. There can *never* be an outside or objective viewpoint. This has serious implications because if you think about it, how can you ever know that you are meditating correctly? You could spend six hours a day for the rest of your life, thinking that you are meditating, without ever actually meditating.

Experienced meditators all speak about moments in meditation in which you *know* within yourself that you have achieved the pure state of meditative mind. Sometimes reaching a few moments of this state can take years on end of practice, or days at a time of meditation. Indeed, some meditators will spend their whole lives meditating and never attain meditative mind. But ultimately the only one who will ever know whether you manage to attain this state or not is yourself.

It was after about five weeks in Thimphu that I came closest to attaining meditative mind. It was an early morning session and the meditation experience itself started like any other. I was sitting cross-legged, back straight, arms and body totally relaxed, feeling the rush of air over my top lip as my lungs drew breath inwards. At the base of my belly I could feel the slow rise and fall as my lungs expanded and contracted. For a moment I was aware of my heart beating steadily and I thought that I could hear the beats echoing in my head. Far away a bird chirped on a roof. Behind all of the other sounds was the sound of silence, enveloping me completely; that peaceful stillness, to which I was becoming accustomed, filling my being. As always I could feel a slight tension behind my eyes, a feeling that I have come to call "clenched mind", and I consciously relaxed and softened this tension, letting it go a little with each out-breath. One or two thoughts arose, like they always did, and when I gradually became aware that they were carrying me away I consciously let them go and returned to the breathing support. So far, it was not unlike any other meditation I had embarked upon.

At some stage (I am not sure exactly when as time loses its measurability during meditation) I slowly became aware that my mind had seemed to tip over into another realm. All sense of dimension and direction had left me and I felt I was suspended in mid-air, miles above my body. It was the strangest sensation I had ever had; almost numb, but at the same time hyper-aware. I felt as if my mind had turned inside out, so that everything outside was inside, and everything inside was out! Lying in a hot bath and then letting the water out while remaining lying there is the type of feeling that I think comes closest to it; as the water drains out, gravity starts to develop around your limbs, and your body feels like it is attaining a type of reality it didn't have before. In the process you experience a new awareness of your being.

I knew only from checking my watch afterwards that the session had lasted for an hour. As far as the actual experience had gone, it might just as well have been ten seconds or a week. Time lost all relevance. What I do remember is what happened to me after the session.

Sam struck the little Tibetan gong and I opened my eyes slowly, very slowly, gradually focusing them on her sitting on the black cushion in front of me. But as her long, dark hair came into focus I saw that it wasn't only Sam sitting on that cushion. She was there, but within her, looking out of her eyes, was another, familiar person not unlike somebody I'd previously encountered as if in some long forgotten dream. It slowly dawned on me who it was. It was the mysterious woman in black who had come into the hospital ward all those years ago, with a book on Chinese philosophy under one arm. And she knew that I knew. And so did Sam.

A few moments later I left the Wisdom Shoppe. On my way out, still entranced by my encounter, I caught sight of the "Do Not Disturb" sign on the door. Only, this time, the last two words were not separate but had become one:

DO NOT DISTURB.
INTUITION

part IV

TRANSCENDENCE

The oppositions of heaven and earth, of spirit and nature, of man and woman, when reconciled, bring about the creation and re-production of life... Opposition creates the need for a bridge. Thus is opposition the natural prerequisite of union: it is a phase to be transcended.

The Pocket I Ching – Richard Wilhelm

This Statement is False

Paradoxes are peculiar things. Many eastern schools of thought (not just the Taoists) treasure a good paradox. The Zen Buddhists in particular focus strongly on paradoxes (or "koan", as they call them). For paradoxes are the proof that logic is limited. And, as logical thinking is viewed by much of eastern thought as a great tyrant, the absurdities contained in paradoxes are used to shake their practitioners free from rational modes of thought. Only by unshackling the chains of reason can a person transcend to a higher state of enlightenment.

Paradoxes come in many forms and guises. They can't all be solved by simply shifting from linear to circular paradigms. However, one commonality they do all share is the muddle of their outer (objective) and inner (subjective) states. They are like the mirrors of language. When you peer into a mirror you see yourself looking back. But who is this mirrored self – the object or the subject?

Take the statement:

This statement is false.

At first appearance this statement appears perfectly fine. That is because at first you tend to look at the statement from outside the system, as an object; as an object, there is nothing wrong with it. The problem comes when you enter the system and "subject" the statement to itself.

The best way to expose this particular paradox is to ask the question: "Is the statement, '*This statement is false*,' true or false?" In so asking, you will gradually see that if the statement is true, then it must by implication be false. But if it is false, then it cannot be true in the first place. But if it is not true in the first place then it cannot be false, and so on. The result? A self-referring loop with an infinitely recurring tangle. By subjecting the object to its own subject, the paradox gets trapped within its own system.

It's not unlike the quip about the brain: *If our brains were simple enough to understand, we would be so stupid that we wouldn't understand them after all.* Again – the self-referring loop. We can pretend to think of our own minds objectively (from outside the system). But in reality we arc trapped inside the system, for the simpler our brains are to observe objectively, the more complicated the observation becomes subjectively. Object and subject are inextricably linked.

Although peering into these mirrors can be confusing (ask any toddler), it can also teach us valuable information about ourselves. It was only a few days after my unusual meditation experience in Thimphu that it slowly dawned on me that my entire Quest had, itself, fallen into a paradoxical trap.

Binary Digits

The whole thing started one morning in the teashop when I was chatting to John. I had been reading the **I Ching** the night before and was contemplating the claim that the entire universe was, ultimately, constructed of only two elements: Yin and Yang. John responded immediately that this should come as no great surprise, because, "all information is heading that way".

I asked him to elaborate and he explained that there was currently a "digital revolution" taking place in the world whereby all information, whether it be music, software programs or even movies, was being converted into digital computer language. This language was constructed out of nothing more than noughts and ones. Indeed the word "bit", John said, was merely an acronym for the words "binary digit". "Binary" like "bi-polar" meant "two". Unlike our decimal system, which has ten different number symbols, the binary number system consists of only two symbols: a one and a nought.

That an all-encompassing phenomenon such as the digital revolution echoed a similar concept to the ancient concept of

Yin and Yang was very pleasing to me. But I probably would not have taken it any further, had John not gone on to draw my attention to a similarity which just couldn't be ignored. John was passionate about his field, and when you started a conversation rolling in the direction of science or maths, he would light up and leap into a highly intellectual dialogue that could last for well over an hour. A lot of what he said was above me, but there were snippets that I caught that were to have great bearing on my Quest.

Having started on the topic of binary mathematics, John went on to talk about the powers of two, and how everything to do with computers always escalated to the powers of two. "Think about it," he said. "You start with 2 Megs of Ram, then you get 4 Megs, then you get 8, 16, 32 and 64. It's always doubled up. It's always multiplied by two! That's the beauty of the binary system – just multiply it all by two."
I privately wondered how John's pupils managed to keep up with him. Presumably he was different in class. Maybe I was just the outlet for all the pent up theoretical stuff he couldn't share with his Bhutanese pupils.
"And that is exactly why," he continued, "back in the old days we used to get the Commodore 64 computer. It was 64 kilobytes! Today 64 Megs – back then 64 kilobytes! And why 64? Because 64 is simply 2 X 2 X 2 X 2 X 2 X 2. Two to the power of six."
It was at that point that my ears started to prick up. The **I Ching** had 64 hexagrams.

But what was to follow was even more intriguing. Leaving the number 64 for a second, John went on to explain how the binary number system, with only two digits (the one and nought) was the logical choice for computers, indeed the *only* choice. "It all boils down to electrical circuits," he said. "They're either on or off – one or zero." To emphasise his point he scribbled what was meant to be an electrical circuit diagram on a pad on the table, and it was only when I glanced at the diagrams that I felt the first jolt of synchronicity. For, on the paper I saw:

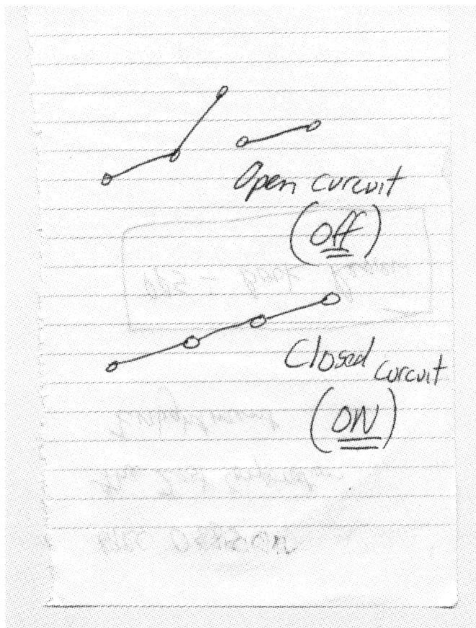

How different was this to:

— — Yin?

And

——— Yang?

Was there a link between computers and the **I Ching**? Was there a link between modern mathematics and Taoist philosophy?

Gottfried Leibniz

Indeed there was. But I was only to expose the link about two days later. Having detected my sudden interest in binary mathematics, John had warmed even more to the subject and went on to give me a run down on the full history. Binary mathematics had been “invented” way back in the 17th century by the great German mathematician, Gottfried Leibniz. I immediately asked John if he knew how Leibniz had come up with the system, but he didn’t. He offered to lend me a book on the history of mathematics.

I collected the book the next day, a really thick volume that was heavy to carry. That night, in my tiny first floor room, I waded through the sizeable section on Leibniz. It didn’t take me that long to find what I was looking for. When I did I jumped for joy around the small guesthouse room.

Originally Leibniz had arrived at the concept of a binary system independently, but had made little progress until a Jesuit monk based in China, with whom he used to correspond, sent him a copy of the **I Ching**. Leibniz was enthralled, immediately recognising the pure brilliance of this binary system, and in his inspired state he went on to perfect his binary mathematics. And it was binary mathematics that led to the modern computer. Leibniz was the first one ever to speak about the possibilities of a "calculating machine." He even drew up a plan for one.

The “Leibniz connection”. Like Pythagoras, Leibniz was actually more a philosopher than a pure mathematician. When he “discovered” binary mathematics he was ecstatic. He believed that the binary system contained not only an algebraic method but an entire cosmological philosophy of the universe. Leibniz vociferously agreed with his predecessor Pythagoras that, “*All is number*”. He even commissioned a large plaque to commemorate his discovery and had a picture of a triangle containing an eye inscribed on the plaque. The triangle, a well known Pythagoric symbol, displayed Leibniz's indebtedness to Pythagoras.

The plaque bore the words:

> *One is enough for deriving everything from nothing - The model of creation discovered by GW Leibniz*

Leibniz believed that his discovery possessed no less than a religious dimension. God, he claimed, represented the one and the zero represented "the void". According to John's book, Leibniz's academic work took a definite change in direction after his discovery and thereafter was described as a "kind of quasi-religious mysticism".

What has a 17th century German philosopher got to do with my Quest? My discoveries did not always unfold in a linear manner (indeed many events overlapped), and relaying them now in a logical order is no easy feat. The week after discovering binary mathematics, my journey took a new turn and only after that was the meaningfulness of the Leibniz connection to become evident.

A Line and a Circle

My time in Thimphu was drawing to an end, and my thoughts had started to turn to the prospect of returning home. In a week or two I would be sitting back behind my desk, fielding calls from my wealthy clients by day and confusing poor Kate by night. It was a world I had left only five weeks earlier but that now seemed so remote. I decided to spend my last weeks consolidating what I had learned. I would use the time to look back on my Quest from its earliest days, and retrace the steps that had brought me to Thimphu.

While I was recalling my journey, a very important thing happened. It was not pre-meditated in any way but simply followed in the natural progression of things. I was sitting at my table with a pen and pad close by and as I considered the differences between my old western way and my new eastern way, I picked up the pen and drew a line down the middle of a page and wrote:

WEST	EAST
WHY	WAY
DIVIDE	DIVINE

REASON	WITHOUT REASON
INTELLECT	INTUITION
MEDICATION	MEDITATION
SEPARATION	HOLISM

The list seemed to be endless and I was still scribbling things down when there was a knock at the door. "Come in," I said irritably, and the son of the owner of the guesthouse poked his head around the door.
"Velly urgent phone call for sir. Velly urgent!"

He beckoned for me to follow him down the stairs to the little lobby. I was annoyed, as I had been right in the middle of my list, but I pulled on some shoes. I was about to leave the room when another important item for inclusion on my list struck me: circular and linear.

My messenger gestured insistently for me to follow him down the stairs but, anxious not to forget about circular and linear, I hastily scribbled a circle under the eastern side of the list, and a straight line under the western side, before descending to the lobby.

The phone call turned out to be from one of my staff members. Between all the echoes and static I gleaned that a client's investment portfolio was rapidly declining on the American stock exchange. I spent the next two hours battling to phone New York, no easy task in this third world country. Frantic conversations ensued between the irate client and the American broker. The guesthouse owner and his son gawked at me as I rattled out buy and sell instructions in US dollars. The phone call seemed surreal in this quaint Bhutanese guesthouse lobby. Once again I was reminded that there was another, very different, life waiting for me out there.

It was only later then, when I returned to my room, sat down once again at the table and looked down at the list I'd made earlier, that the profound significance of what I had done struck me. *Uncanny*! There, before my eyes, under the WEST column was the digit one, and under the EAST column, the digit nought.

For an instant I presumed that in my rush to the door I had somehow lost my thread of thought and had purposely inserted Leibniz's binary digits (which were still fresh in my mind) into the columns. But then I remembered that I had done nothing of the sort. I had simply drawn the simplest and most obvious symbols for a circular system and a linear system!

Zero

For one who had spent the previous six months analysing the divine significance of seemingly random coincidences, an event like this was mind-blowing. Instantly I was on the lookout for hidden meanings. Was the similarity between a circle and zero, and a straight line and one, randomly coincidental? Or did this "slip" have a message for me buried in its depths?

I knew how much symbolism could be contained in the shape of one letter. Was there a link between circles and zeros? After all, numerals are nothing other than the letters of mathematics. Could they hold mystical revelations too?

Following this train of thought, I came upon the next obvious question: Could it be that the eastern way was somehow related to zero?

There had always been an aspect to Sam's teachings that had seemed to elude me, but suddenly, from this new viewpoint, things started slotting into place. After all, was this whole idea of *letting everything go* not simply an attempt to achieve nothingness? For if you let everything go what would you be left with, other than zero? And hadn't Sam spoken of *meditation without a meditator*? What would this be other than *zero meditator*? And wasn't meditation itself simply the attempt to achieve *zero* thought? The more I thought about it, the more the same pattern emerged. Just as Descartes's, "*I think, therefore I am*", had become the cornerstone of western philosophy, the eastern reply of, "*I meditate, therefore I am not*", could well be the cornerstone of eastern philosophy.

I turned my excitement to the **Tao te Ching** to see if I could find any confirmation of my suspicions. I found it all over the place:

> *It* (the Tao) *is like the eternal* <u>*void*</u>
>
> *Seamless, unnamable*
> *It returns to the realm of* <u>*nothing*</u>
>
> *We shape clay into a pot*
> *but it is the* <u>*emptiness*</u> *inside*
> *that holds whatever we want*
>
> *We hammer wood for a house*
> *But it is the inner space*
> *that makes it livable*
>
> *We work with being*
> *But* <u>*non-being*</u> *is what we use*

Being is born of non-being

Look, and it can't be seen
Listen, and it can't be heard
Reach, and it can't be grasped.

After several hours immersed in the sacred text, I was convinced that the Tao *was* zero. Nothingness. Emptiness. The void. The Way was not only the Way of a circle, it was the Way of zero.

Nothingness is a bizarre proposition. We tend to take it for granted. But have you ever actually seen or experienced nothingness? Indeed, can nothingness exist? If we sent out a team of the top hundred scientists in the world and said, "You've got ten years to find nothing", – would they find it? Could they find it? After all, even vacuums are full of waves and particles. I soon arrived at a new appreciation for the cliché, "Nothing is impossible".

Being raised in an affluent western culture, the value of "nothing" as opposed to "something" is difficult to grasp. In a society consumed with materialism we have been brought up to place great value on "things". The corollary of "things" is "no-things", so it shouldn't come as any great surprise that "nothing" is attributed zero value. The void has always been regarded in a negative light. It is associated with death, blackness and evil. You just have to look etymologically at the word "naughty" to appreciate the way in which we perceive naught. We celebrate birth and mourn death, believing the two to be totally unrelated. Yet as the **Tao te Ching** puts it:

Each separate being in the universe
returns to the common source.

Where we come from, is where we return. "*From ashes to ashes, dust to dust*" is misleading. It should rather read from "*nothingness to nothingness*". The common source. "Nothingness" is the womb of life. It is the "*emptiness within the pot*", rather than the pot itself, which sustains the essence of being.

ERROR

Fortunately I still had John's book on the history of mathematics with me. I needed to delve deeper into the roots of zero. Where did this nothingness come from? Did the history of zero hold some crucial clues? Perhaps in days to come zero would prove to be as central to my Quest as the letter Y had? After all, was it not Y that had led me to zero in the first place?

Once again, the book showed the way. Of the ten digits we use today, zero was the last to be incorporated and also possesses the most checkered history of the numerals. As with the alphabet's history, there was no precise answer for where zero originally sprang from. All agreed, however, that the east was the chief protagonist in its development. The Indians in particular had always been great mathematicians and if there was one country where zero seemed to be most rooted it was undoubtedly India.

This fascinated me and I dug out **The Eastern Way**, another book I had bought from the Wisdom Shoppe, which contained a fairly large section on Hinduism. It wasn't long before I came across the Hindu equivalent of Tao: Brahman. Like the Tao, Brahman was the ultimate reality, formless and seamless, but ever present beneath the surface of all things. It, too, was compared to the void. But what excited me the most was that Brahman went by many names and two such names, "akasa" and "purna", were also two of the names originally used to describe the new mathematical number – zero!

Like the round earth view, zero was greeted with great disdain by the medieval Church. This number was a direct challenge to the nature of God, undoubtedly the work of the devil, the cardinals claimed. Leibniz had been fortunate that, having broken the universe into ones and zeros, he had chosen the one to represent God. Had he chosen zero, his story might well not have reached us.

But opposition was not confined to Europe. When zero first appeared in India it also met considerable suspicion. The primary objection was that zero seemed to contain within itself a ridiculous paradox: how could you talk about anything that was both "something" and "nothing" at the same time, the conservatives asked. For if "nothing" was nothing, how could it possibly simultaneously be "something"?

I snapped my fingers triumphantly when I learnt of this Indian paradox. Suddenly it linked zero with Y, Osiris and puns. For here was another entity with "dual nature" written all over it. Like an almighty forked tongue, zero proclaimed to the world that it was something, when, in reality, it was nothing. Zero was the Osiris of mathematical numerals, straddling the worlds of being and non-being. Here, lurking in this ultimate of double binds, was the link between zero and my Quest.

The final proof came to me via the most logical route possible: a mathematical proof. For zero, after all, is a number, and no analysis of this concept would be complete without examining its mathematical properties. You don't have to be a mathematical genius to get to where I am going; the cheapest of pocket calculators will do.

In most respects zero is like any other number. You can add, subtract and multiply any number by zero. But the minute you try to divide anything by zero you come up with a serious problem. Punch any number in, divide it by zero and, there on the screen, you will not get a number, but rather a word: ERROR. At last I had found the concrete proof I sought: *according to zero, division is erroneous!*

This wasn't the only mathematical proof I discovered. Another common viewpoint of all eastern philosophies is that the ultimate reality (or "God") is everywhere present. Once again, zero passes the algebraic test with flying colours. This time addition is used; when zero is added to any number the answer is always equal to that number. For example: 3 + 0 = 3. Therefore, if you put it the other way around: every number *already contains zero*! 3 already contains 0, because 3 = 3 + 0. So does 105 678 contain zero for 105 678 = 105 678 + 0. So zero is ever present in every number in the universe. Or as the **Tao te Ching** puts it:

> *That which has no substance*
> *Enters where there is no space.*

When I finally put my head down on my pillow that night I was on a high. My enlightenment was complete, I thought with triumph! I had arrived at a profound insight into the workings of the Tao which few westerners (or even easterners!) ever understood. I had solved the riddle of the cosmos and, from hereon after, everything was going to make perfect sense. I could *see things as they actually were*. Before blowing out the flame of the butter lamp I took my pen and below the straight line and the circle in the WEST and EAST columns of my list, I wrote "One" and "Zero".

Vicious Circle

The next day I should have awakened to bliss and enlightenment. But the day that presented itself was to prove anything but blissful. It started when I first surfaced, groggy and gritty eyed (which I suppose was not surprising considering that I had only got to sleep around 3am). I lay in bed, accustoming my eyes to the dappled shafts of sunlight, before rolling over and catching sight of my pad on the bedside table. I picked it up and stared at the two columns I had written out the day before.

WEST	EAST
WHY	WAY
DIVIDE	DIVINE

REASON	WITHOUT REASON
INTELLECT	INTUITION
MEDICATION	MEDITATION
SEPARATION	HOLISM
	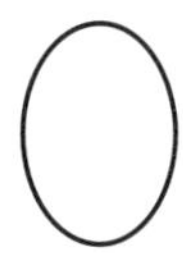
ONE	ZERO

As I looked at the list something stirred deep within me; the distant memory of writing a similar list fifteen years previously: the same line down the middle; oppositions listed on either side. The list that I now held in my hand, and the list that I'd written the day I entered hospital in 1984, were almost identical. Lists of duality, lists of separation between universal polarities.

Something very wrong was contained in this realisation. Had the whole purpose of my Quest, and specifically my trip to the east, not been to escape dualism and division? Had my mission not been to view the world in a new, holistic way so that the illusion of separation was dissolved? Were the contents of this new list in my hand *really* the culmination of enlightened insight?

Instead of having an either black or white problem on my hands, I now had an either west or east problem on my hands. Why or Way, one or zero, all or nothing – it was the *same* problem. I had come back to that same unbridgeable chasm: the same either/or tree. Far from transcending the diabolical horns of my dilemma, I had merely become impaled on a sharper and more far-reaching horn. I had come full circle. Only this circle, instead of being a circle of all encompassing enlightenment, was a vicious circle!

The night before, I had believed that my enlightenment would surely cure the mid-life depression that had sparked this whole Quest. Now I realised my foolishness. The prospect of returning to the clouds of meaninglessness in South Africa loomed large. There wasn't a light at the end of the tunnel after all. In fact, the tunnel didn't have an end, it just went round and round and round in never-ending circles. As I popped the Prozac into my mouth that morning, I felt a renewed bond with the little green and white pill; maybe we still had a long road to travel together.

After breakfast I strode down the sidewalk to the Wisdom Shoppe. Perhaps Sam would have an answer for me – some magical solution that would make this latest dilemma disappear. But there had been unusually little activity on the streets that day and only when I saw the "Closed" sign on the door did I remember that it was a Bhutanese public holiday. I examined the sign closely to see if there was some way to contact Sam, but there wasn't. All it said, underneath "Closed", were the words:

Proprietor: Samsara D Rampochee.

Suddenly it dawned on me how little I actually knew about Sam. I didn't even know where she lived. For the first time in ages I felt really, really alone. I rushed over to the teahouse to see if John was about, but that too was closed for the public holiday.

When I got back to my room in the guesthouse I searched frantically through my book on general eastern philosophy. If the answer was not in the Tao, then perhaps it could be found elsewhere in the east?

It was in the section on Buddhism that I came across the Buddhist concept of *samsara.* Sam was a shortened version of the name Samsara. But this name contained a horrible coincidence, for "samsara", in the Buddhist philosophy, was the endless wheel of life, death and rebirth from which the Buddhists believed we humans can never escape. Samsara, in other words, is the ultimate vicious circle, and this was the circle in which my whole Quest now appeared to be trapped. There was no way out.

Looking at the cursed list again, with the glaring one and zero, I realised that these two numbers represented my personal *digital divide*. No longer did the circle represent a healing holism but rather, a mighty loophole. For it appeared now that there was a great *hole* within the whole. *The spell was in the spelling*! No wonder the word holism was spelt without a "w".

As I pondered zero's loophole, I wondered what Sam would say about it. Maybe she would laugh at me and say, "But that is exactly what zero is – a hole within a whole. Zero *is* the loophole!" And in her imagined laughter I detected a strangely grim ring of truth.

The River

I had lost my Way in Bhutan. I had now landed myself in the biggest paradox of them all, the paradox that non-dualism (i.e. holism) was itself part of an even greater dualism. From within (subjectively), the all-inclusive nature of the Tao looked great. But now, examining the Tao from the outside (objectively), I could see that non-dualism, by definition, excluded dualism, which in itself *created* a dualism (the dualism between non-dualism and dualism). Instead of being trapped within an either/or dualism I was now trapped in an *either* dualism *or* non-dualism. It was the same almighty Y-junction. What was the difference?

That night I tossed and turned for ages before falling asleep. When sleep finally came, it was charged with powerful and vivid dreams. I dreamt that I was somewhere near a large river looking for something. What exactly it was, I did not know, but I knew it was proving difficult to find and I knew that I was getting frustrated.

Just then, a man appeared. John. He pointed upstream. “That is where you will find what you are looking for,” he said, in his distinguished Cambridge accent. I followed his advice and ventured up along the banks of the river. But I didn't find anything there and after a while I retraced my steps to where I had started.

Then a woman appeared. Samsara. "Why are you angry?" she asked.
“I can't find what I'm looking for. John swore I'd find it further upstream. But it wasn't there.”
“Don't be angry, young friend. Upstream is wrong. What you seek is only found downstream.”
I followed the river down along its banks but couldn't see anything.

Then the dream got blurred and somehow I arrived back at where I had started. But now John and Samsara were both there, arguing with each other. The argument got quite heated and I was about to intervene when the rock I was standing on toppled and I fell into the river. I panicked. But then I felt the cool water around me and suddenly I felt really good. I knew intuitively that I had found what I was looking for.

Time

I awakened. And that is how I discovered the folly of my entire Quest. The river in the dream represented *time*. John, who had pointed upstream, was trying to tell me that the answers I was seeking lay in the past. But they didn't. Then Samsara came and was trying to tell me that my answers lay in the future, downstream. But she was also to be proved wrong.

Of all the words and concepts that I have researched in the dictionary, “time” is the one that eludes definition. It is unarguably one of the most difficult concepts to comprehend. We think that in our great technological advancement we are able to track time with our clocks and stopwatches. But think about it; if time decided to speed up of its own accord, wouldn’t our clocks and stopwatches simply speed up too? 1 o'clock would still be 1 o'clock and 6 o'clock, 6. Would we even know the difference?

Imagine a universe without time. Imagine we could record the whole of life on planet earth as we know it, onto a giant video recording and then take ourselves out of the system and sit back and watch the video. Now imagine we push the pause button… Everything stops! Jumbo jets stop dead in the sky. Raindrops stop in mid-air. Lights stop flickering. Pistons in car engines suddenly freeze in precise positions. Rivers cease flowing. The earth stops spinning on its axis. Our hearts refrain from beating...

Time is clearly integral to any religion, philosophy or wisdom that attempts to find the ultimate meaning of life. It was only after dreaming about John and Samsara and the river, that it struck me that contained within my Quest was an enormous problem.

While trapped in my western perspective of things and continually searching for the great “*Why?*”, I was, of necessity, continually looking backwards at only one dimension of time – the past. That is how science and reason work; they look for causes, for provable events and these, if you analyse them, can only exist in the past. *The proof of the pudding is in the eating*, and the pudding must always already have been cooked. Upstream, with John; the scientists' domain.

Reasons also inhabit the past. Psychiatrists and psychologists love the past, the further back the better, and they encourage clients to vigorously re-visit their past experiences. The beginning of my Quest, when I look at it now, was forever looking backwards, scouring ancient lands and eternally stuck in the days of 1984. Eternally pointing fingers at parents and childhood. I am not saying there are no clues in the past. But how can we ever know where we are going if our cars are built with the headlights at the back of the car so that we focus on where we are coming from?

Knowing where we are going is where divination comes in. Trying to discern the future, trying to find the correct path up ahead. How do you find the Way? By looking in front of you, not behind. Consulters of the **I Ching** are always concerned with the future – with which way to go.

Of course, what is in front of us can never be known. It remains hidden, yet to unfold. Reason, therefore, is hopelessly inadequate to guide us forward. Intuition is far more attuned to the future. The artist is always free to draw pictures of the future, whereas the scientist, trapped behind the lens of his technological camera, can never capture the future. Its subject matter is forever out of reach.

When I first discovered the Way in Bhutan, I believed that all of my answers lay in this new dimension of time. Just as the thesis of "why" was backward thinking, the thesis of "way" was forward thinking. Forward thinking was much more harmonious with getting somewhere in my Quest, and I reasoned that to focus on the future made far more sense. After all, I had thought, *the future was where I was going to spend the rest of my life.*

But this "future thinking" also had a flaw in it; a massive flaw. If the problem was simply a case of my answers not being located downstream in my dream, as Samsara had said, it wouldn't be so bad. But the problem is much more serious than that.

The problem is that Samsara might not exist.

There, I've said it. Not only might Samsara not exist, but I have never been to Bhutan. My whole pilgrimage to the east has been set *in the future*. In that sense it has been fictitious. While telling you about the Wisdom Shoppe, I have, if the truth be told, been sitting in my study in Durban, a busy financial advisor by day, and a budding storyteller by night.

The Now

A paradox worthy of eastern mystics springs to mind as I make this confession: "I am a liar". But is it true?

Before I am labelled deceitful and a cheat, let me explain a few things. Besides my time in Thimphu, this story is the truth. Although Samsara and John are fictitious characters, what I have said about the history of mathematics, and the quotes I have included from the Chinese classics, are historically accurate. But perhaps most importantly – I *have* been in tuition. I've been in tuition with my own intuition. Many long hours have I spent each day in real meditation. And experiencing the Now – I like to think – is partly how I have arrived at most of my insights.

I say "partly", because this process of writing, too, has been instrumental in my journey. Being prepared to release my Quest from pure reason, to play with ideas, to give free rein to my imagination, to blur the line between fact and fiction – these have all contributed to my insights. For, I have begun to ask, why do we feel the need for this apartheid style separation between fact and fiction? Why should experiences always be neatly boxed and categorised? Is fiction inferior to non-fiction? Need the two always be mutually exclusive?

I *am*, after all, planning a trip to the east. And for all we know, I may well meet Samsara. From all you have read of her, for all she has given to me, would you be prepared to swear that she does not exist? What *is* real, after all?

As the eastern sages always proclaim, the real journey of intuition is the journey within. It is not necessary to jump on an aeroplane in order to participate in the journey of intuition. Was it not the **Tao te Ching** that said:

> *Without looking out your window*
> *You can see the essence of the Tao.*

My dream of the river drew my attention to an almighty blindspot in my Quest. It made me aware, for the first time, that if I really do want to get off Prozac, and solve my life-long problems, I need to get into (or perhaps fall into) the river of time right *where I am*. Because, spending your time searching in the future for the Way is just as futile as searching in the past for the Why. The place to live is in the *Now* – not in the past or future. *The only all-inclusive moment of time is the Now.*

In the **Tao te Ching** there is a verse, "*The journey of a thousand miles starts from under your feet*". Few people know this saying in its original form. It has been corrupted over the years into the better known, "*The journey of a thousand miles starts with a single step*". This "alteration" is subtle and seems insignificant, yet what the **Tao te Ching** was saying in its original form was that any journey in life starts even before the first step. It starts in the Now – in the present moment where you are, *wherever* that might be. By delaying the journey until "the first step", you are deferring the journey out of the Now, because "the first step" automatically becomes part of the future.

I had been avoiding the Now for this entire Quest. The solution always seemed to lie in my life fifteen years before, or else in the future in Bhutan. What really needed fixing was my life in Durban today. For all her nagging, Kate was right! How could I talk about transcendence and enlightenment when I wasn't even facing the problems of my current existence?

Dr Jekyll and Mr Hyde

For a long time now, I had been living a double life. In the one life, I'd been living in Bhutan, consumed with this Quest. But still linked to that self was the financial advisor, the down-to-earth, trustworthy guy to whom the public entrusted their millions. And these two selves were miles and miles apart.

So one part of me went one way
And the other part went a bit stray
As the days went by, each part
Grew further and further apart
We seem to have lost each other forever
When will I be together?

I still was not together. The link remained missing. The poem I had written fifteen years before held not only the secrets of the past but the secrets of the future too, the secrets of *Now*.

Am I a go-getter
A trendy jet-setter?
Or am I just mellow
A quiet, content fellow?

I still didn't know. Yuppie financial advisor or mystical esoteric philosopher? Dr Jekyll or Mr Hyde? Two lives: a daytime life and a night-time life, each tightly compartmentalised from the other, each self carrying within it the dark secret of the other self.

And what of my relationship with Kate? Where was it going? "How could it have a future," it dawned on me with guilt and sadness, "when it has so little present?"

Perhaps this whole Quest had been a lie. Perhaps the Y actually stood for me. "*I* am the pun," I thought, "that says one thing to the world and means entirely another! *I* am the letter that masquerades as a consonant by day, but is actually a vowel by night! *I* am the Osiris who lives straddled between the worlds of my two selves, each world so many light years apart from the other. And", I figured, "all this time that I have been pointing at the divining rod, the divining rod has actually been pointing right back at *me*!"

The Dialectic

A period of despondency followed my realisation. If my Quest had achieved anything in this past year it was to show me that I really had made no progress in fifteen years. I was still a divided individual with a split mind. And although this Schizophrenia was not certifiable, in a way it was even more dishonest than my 1984 state of mind.

For days I dragged myself to the office, performing the bare minimum to keep the business ticking over. My staff asked me if everything was alright. Kate grew more and more silent, the gulf of misery growing ever wider between us. During the evenings I'd lock myself in my study and sit, surrounded by piles of books. But no more insights came. It was all pointless. A wretched cycle of suffering to which we had to resign ourselves. An urban congestion of recycled junk. Meaningless. Arbitrary.

Which route would I follow? Where would I be tomorrow?
Unfortunately I lacked the precision to make such a decision…

It was the Y that saved me. One evening I sat in my study, a mug of *rooibos* tea steaming on the desk. It had been a long day at work and I was paging through an old philosophy text book, not really looking at the pages, but just flipping them for want of something better to do. My mind had become dull and lethargic and I spent a lot of time just staring into space. The Prozac didn't seem to be working.

SIGN OF THE TIMES

“Good Lord Deliver Us.” I started. That was the sound of the fiery-necked nightjar, calling across the valley. At that precise moment, as I was jerked out of my reverie, a diagram on one of the pages caught my eye. For a second the lethargy lifted. I stopped flipping the pages and backtracked to the diagram: GW Hegel’s Dialectic.

A German philosopher who lived at the turn of the 18th century, Hegel developed an elaborate philosophy that came to represent a whole era in philosophy known as “the age of the system”. The bulk of Hegel’s philosophical work was extremely obscure. He started out as more of a mystic than an analytical philosopher. Much of his inspiration came from a largely unknown German shoemaker of the 17th century, Jakob Boehme.

Boehme was a Christian mystic who prayed so ardently and persistently that one day a ray of light reflecting off a pewter bowl struck him, and for seven days the divine secrets of the entire universe were said to be revealed unto him. Although this mystical encounter placed Boehme on the wrong side of the contemporary Church, it did earn him a small place in history as a 17th century mystic. (Luckily for him, he was not in the South African Defence Force during his seven days of revelation!)

Like the great thinkers of the east, Hegel believed that all things in the universe were connected.[20] He proclaimed emphatically that things could only be understood in their relationship with the whole. “The true is the whole,” was his undying mantra. He was particularly interested in the interplay between opposites in the history of thought, and it is this process that he called the “dialectic”.

His starting point for the dialectic was a thesis. Which thesis wasn’t important; it was the process that mattered, not the particulars. In time any thesis, said Hegel, would always (and without exception) attract an antithesis contradicting the first

[20] The irony is that although Hegel's philosophies have often been likened to eastern philosophies, Hegel himself derided the Chinese, believing their civilisation to be far inferior to his Prussian state.

thesis. This state of contradiction would cause a certain amount of tension, creating a "mental energy field" between the opposites. The build up of energy would eventually give birth to a psychic spark and, with this, a new *synthesis* of the thesis and antithesis would come into being.

The synthesis (which was itself a thesis), would transcend the contradiction inherent in the previous two theses, resulting in a more enlightened thesis. Opposites within this system were, therefore, the essential ingredient, because it was the interplay between the opposites that created the dynamo for transcendence.

Interesting to me was that the act of transcendence produces a third element (the synthesis) and not merely a compromised position between the thesis and the antithesis. When dealing with conflicting viewpoints, the suggestion is usually to seek middle ground and reach the golden mean. But the mere compromise between black and white invariably leads to a stagnant gray. And stagnant gray is not what transcendence is about. Transcendence does not seek middle ground; rather, it seeks *higher* ground. It seeks something outside of the existing system.

It was here that the Y came in. For the diagram of Hegel's Dialectic, contained none other than the Pythagorean letter.

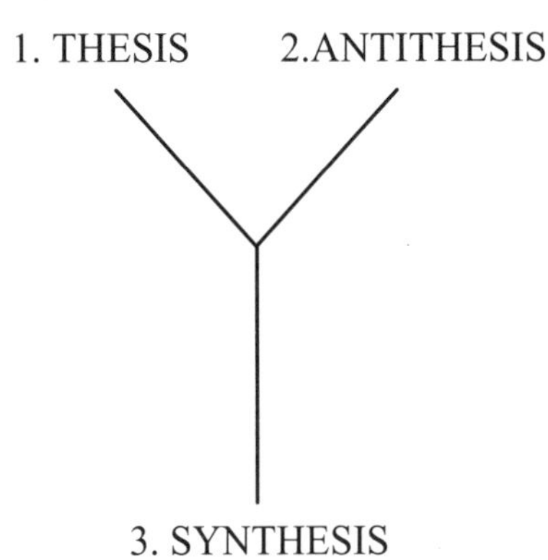

There is, however, an important difference between Hegel's and Pythagoras's letters. The difference is not to be found in the shape of the letter, but rather in the direction from which it is approached. According to Pythagoras, when faced with the letter Y, you had to approach it from the single path before reaching the point where it splits into two. This splitting is where the problem arises, because now you would have two paths in front of you and you would have to choose only one. An *either/or* choice would have to be made.

Hegel's letter, on the other hand, starts with the two prongs of the Y and converges into one. Instead of either/or we have something totally new. We now have a synthesis, a third element that is partly *both* of the previous two prongs but at the same time, partly *neither*. According to Hegel, Pythagoras had the *wrong end of the stick*!

Maybe I, too, had been approaching my problems the wrong way? It's always been *analysis, analysis, analysis. Synthesis*, as any good dictionary will tell you, is the opposite of analysis.

What I really needed to be doing, I realised with growing excitement, was finding a new place where both the *quiet content fellow* and the *go-getter* could bring out their respective bests. Where my imagination at play was not confined, hermit-like, to night-time hours in my locked study, but was allowed to spill over and breath new life into my public self, my daytime existence, my relationship with Kate. Where there was room for both the fiction of Bhutan and the harder facts of modern day South Africa. Where the straitjacket sanity of contemporary life and the freewheeling insanity of Ward 24 needn't exclude each other. And where the conscious and unconscious minds could be in synch – a synthesis between western medication and eastern meditation.

Now, forced to face the present, I realised that depression was not my real problem. Depression was just a symptom of the real problem, which was Schizophrenia. And the division that was causing the Schizophrenia was not located in some mystical trance in the back seat of a car fifteen years previously, but was right here and now. It was a direct consequence of living the Schizophrenic reality of modern life; it was the result of adjusting *too well* to the deeply dualistic, two-faced society into which I had been born.

And perhaps the most important schism I needed to transcend was that between my mother and my father. After all, I am their living synthesis, between my father's tendency towards rigid rationality and my mother's bias towards unpragmatic intuition. They might well be thesis and antithesis, but it is I who needs to bring them together in myself. After all, if I can't do that then, "*When will I be together?*"

Two Paths Converging

Searching for synthesis is not always easy. In some ways it is like searching for rainbows. For rainbows occur when there is a coincidence (coming together) of opposing weather: black weather (rain) and white weather (sun). Only when the weather enters that bizarre state traditionally known as "the monkey's wedding", and is momentarily caught up in this either/or dilemma, can this third element be given birth. And far from being a stagnant grey, this third element transcends the whole black/white dichotomy. From the rainbow an entire spectrum of colour blossoms. And what better symbol of transcendence than the divine arch?

As hard as they are to find, rainbows do occur. Back on 16 March 1994, I hadn't even commenced with this Quest. But that morning, as I sat at my desk in my office, eager to scan the financial markets, a prophetic clue had appeared. A strange tingle went up my spine as I unfurled the morning paper. Across the front page, emblazoned in bold green, was a mighty branch of wisdom. The new South African flag had been unfurled.

That day, I wasn't totally appreciative of the words written in the article below. But I still have a copy of that newspaper (why I kept it at the time, I'll never knew.) And today those words are what I've been looking for all along.

> *The new national symbol represents the two paths (of black and white people) converging and then proceeding on the same path.*

Your life tells you your path if you stop to look at the clues it has been throwing at you all of this time.

* * *

Metamorphosis

A year has passed since I visited Bhutan. The impasse between financial advisor and mystic philosopher could not continue so I decided to sell up everything. It was with fear and trepidation that I presented my decision to Kate. For the first time in a long time, I saw the Kate of earlier times; her face lit up, the wide, almost impish grin I loved so much stretched across her face, she leapt up from the couch and threw her slender arms around me, hugging me with surprising strength. She was enthused! How I had underestimated her!

In a matter of weeks it was all gone: the luxury house, the fancy Cabriolet, and the financial consultancy. I packed away the suits and ties. I bid farewell to my faithful staff. And I prepared to move on. Perpetuating the lie wasn't doing anybody any good. What was the point of having the *means* to live if your life had no *mean*ing?

THE NATAL MERCURY
NATAL NEWSPAPERS •• WEDNESDAY MARCH 16, 1994 R1,00 (incl. VAT) Subscriptions from 80c (Where available)

Dual anthems in the interim

SA's new flag unfurled

By Donwald Pressly
Political Reporter

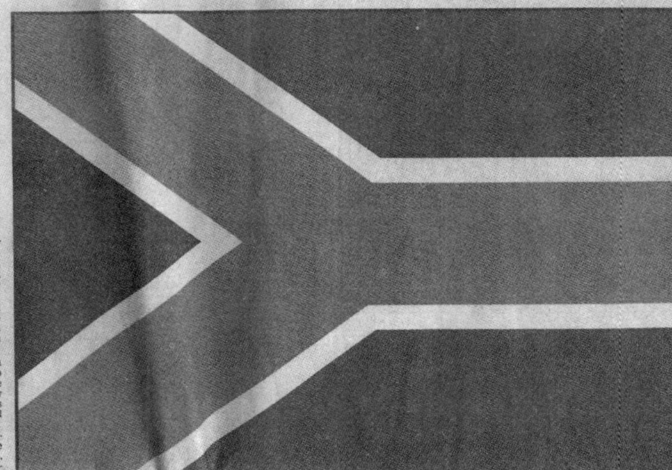

PRETORIA—South Africa has a new flag.

Representing a horizontal Y in six colours — red, green, blue, white, black and gold — it will probably fly for the first time when parliament sits 10 days after the April poll.

The TEC revealed the flag — which will last for the five-year transitional period — and also chose *Die Stem* and *Nkosi Sikelel 'iAfrika* as the interim national anthems, on the recommendation of constitutional development minister Roelf Meyer and ANC secretary-general Cyril Ramaphosa.

The two, who formed a sub-committee to study 7 000 flag proposals submitted by the public, emphasised that it was an interim flag which could be changed by the new constituent assembly.

The new national symbol includes some of the official colours of the National Party (red, white and blue), the ANC (black, green and gold), the South African Communist Party (Red) and even the Democratic Party

Mr Meyer said this was a winning factor in selecting it, while Mr Brownwell, who played a crucial role in the creation of the independence flag of Namibia, said the new national symbol represented the two paths (of black and white people) converging "and then proceeding on the same path".

Vierkleur of the Boer Republic (red, green, and white) — as well as those looking forward, he said.

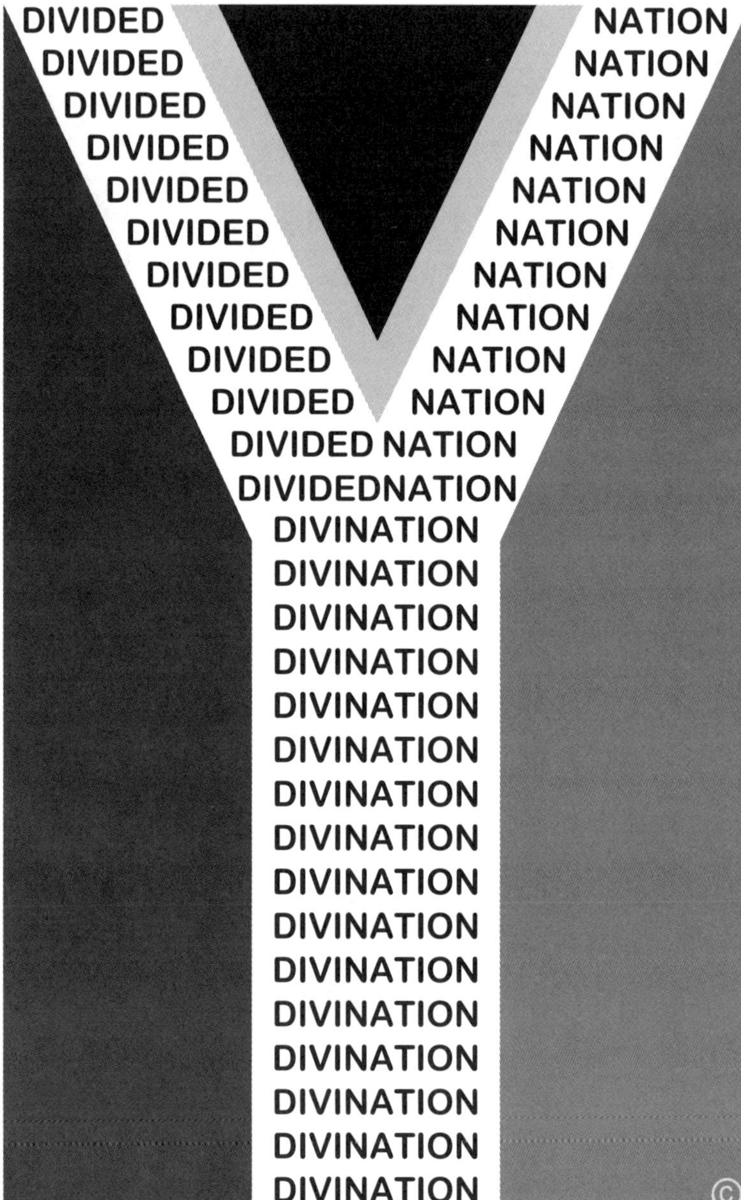
DIVIDED
NATION
DIVIDED
NATION
DIVIDED
NATION
DIVIDED
NATION
DIVIDED
NATION
DIVIDED
NATION
DIVIDED
NATION
DIVIDED
NATION
DIVIDED
NATION
DIVIDED
NATION
DIVIDED NATION
DIVIDEDNATION
DIVINATION
DIVINATION
DIVINATION
DIVINATION
DIVINATION
DIVINATION
DIVINATION
DIVINATION
DIVINATION
DIVINATION
DIVINATION
DIVINATION
DIVINATION
DIVINATION
DIVINATION
DIVINATION
©

We now live in a seaside village in the Cape of Good Hope. Kate loves me, it seems, for who I really am; no longer do I need the Yuppie, Conqueror-of-the-World pretence. She loves my body *and* my mind and is fascinated by my Quest. But then again, I allow her to be part of it. No longer am I dogged by the shame of division, the stark fraudulence of a daytime self and a night-time self. No longer do I feel the need to play separate roles to please different audiences.

"Oh, Chris," she says, in her characteristically calm, incisive way, "here's one for you". She's sitting curled up in an armchair in the lounge, next to a roaring log fire in our new home. One hand rests gently on the glossy, black fur of our latest "joint venture", a puppy. The other holds the book from which she now reads aloud. I put aside my own book, on the French post-modernist thinkers, for a moment abandoning Derrida and his fascination with puns, while I listen. "This is from someone by the name of Roethke, Theodore Roethke, apparently a poet. Listen to this: 'We learn by going / Where we have to go.' Pretty profound, huh?"

She leaves for work in the city each day, and I wave her off, then return to the quiet, contemplative space of my study. I guess I'm just as intense as ever, and just as prone to question everything I come across. But our lives have changed. My energy is no longer as destructive. She no longer feels the burden of being "the sensible one" in our little circle of existence. We grow our vegetables. We walk barefoot on the dunes, the bleached Atlantic sand tickling our toes. We cycle to the local store when we need basic provisions.

We spend time, not money. Things are simpler. *Now.*

On the other side of the bay from us live my mom, dad and sister. Surprisingly enough, perhaps, it was my dad who discovered this tranquil seaside village. He has in the past years been consumed with his own art: photography.[21] It was while scouting one day for interesting landscape subjects that he came upon this beautiful bay and rugged dunes. You know, he's changed a lot, my dad. Nowadays, it humbles me to see the sheer beauty and creativity of his photos, which are also (needless to say perhaps), technically brilliant! "Proof that people aren't doomed to stay trapped in their characteristic ways of being," I always think. It comes home to me very forcefully, when I look at my dad nowadays, that we humans have this unique ability to change and grow.

Not a week goes by that I don't walk across the beach to visit my family. There is still the usual squabbling in the household but strangely we are very close, the four of us. We share an unusually deep bond that has somehow emerged out of all the years of pain and discord. I'm thankful I will be sharing my parents' golden years with them.

I'm not sure what you would call what I now do for a living. My new business card says:

the WORD *project*
©hristopher

digital art, prose, philosophy
www.thewordproject.com

Digital Art wasn't a career path that I consciously chose. It just seemed to come to me. I'd always tinkered around with various computer graphic design programs. After all, Kate's work in packaging meant that she was immersed in this kind of technology. Then one night I was doodling around with an animation program and I found that I could create words that metamorphosed into other words. By altering the angle of perspective of various letters in my artworks, I discovered that I could join previously polarised concepts: up and down, north and south, east and west.

[21] My dad took the cover photo for this book on a recent photographic trip.

East and west was particularly relevant, as my artwork not only served to join the two terms, but went further to show that east and west were actually one and the same thing. They just looked different when viewed from different points of view. They were relative rather than absolute.

The further I explored words and concepts, the more subtle were the links I discovered. Little coincidences that make you take notice and think. Most people don't see them. We are so caught up in the meanings of words that often we can no longer *see them as they actually are.*

Take the clichés that I've used throughout this text. We are so accustomed to their metaphorical meaning that we have to really focus to appreciate what the words are actually saying.

Beneath their meanings are shapes and patterns that paint their own pictures and realities. And the way these shapes and patterns interact carries its own message. Sometimes this message is in agreement with the literal messages and you get a profound tautology where the words *say what they are and are what they say*. Other times you get paradoxes; weird, mind-bending paradoxes that can captivate you for hours – not unlike the koan by which Zen monks are so mesmerised.

I suppose in a way my art is really a giant synthesis for me. It brings previously fragmented things together: art and language; word and image; precision and imagination. Language can feel like a very linear medium; each word, each sentence, each book, has a beginning and an end. They're all sequential. But for me, images are different. They are more circular in their representation of the world. The whole can be absorbed "all at once". I like to think that through the melding of word and image, the circular and linear are synthesised in the art pieces I do. This is not out of line with the etymology of "art" which goes back to an Indo-European root **ar-*, meaning "put things together, join".[22]

---

[22] **The Dictionary of Word Origins**

POINTS OF VIEW:
EAST & WEST

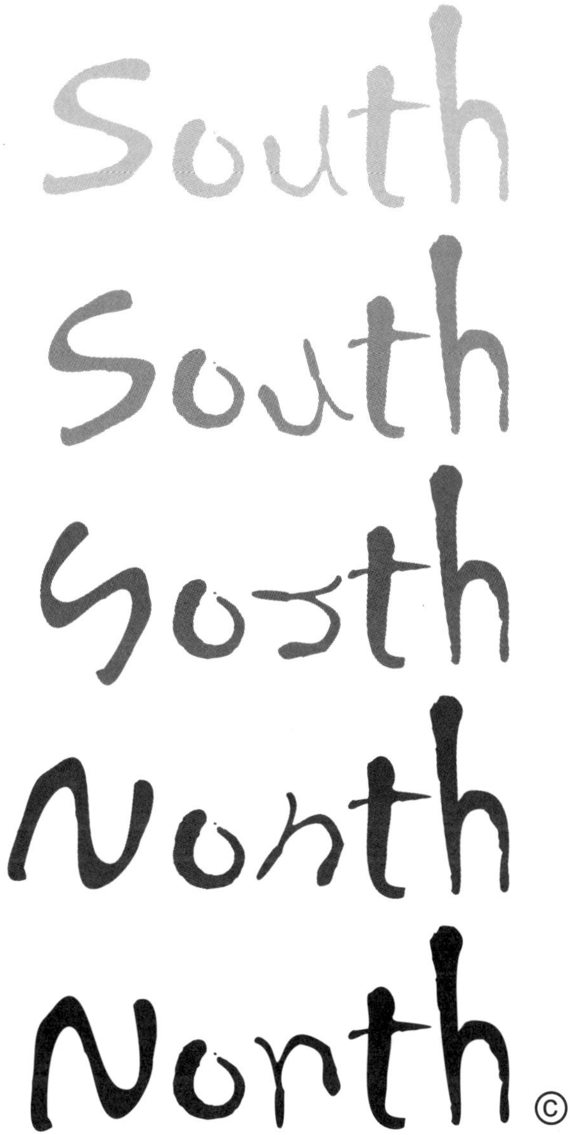

**POINTS OF VIEW:
POLES APART**

While doing my art I often experience an intense excitement. At times it is very like the feeling I had back in the bad old days of 1984 – on the back seat of the car that night, and then subsequently in hospital and in Ward 24. It's that same incongruous mix of trance and heightened awareness. Just like back then, I feel the excitement of being in the grip of some magical power. But now I am free to follow it, to let it linger, to embrace and celebrate it.

For the past 6 months I've been putting together a vast website ***(www.thewordproject.com)*** where my animated pieces can hang out. I've included some of the pieces in this book, but they really need to be seen in their animated form. The art comes alive with animation. The world wide web is my stage and the characters of my keyboard play out all sorts of scripts on this international platform. In this world, I am an almighty Creator, breathing the breath of life into my character's nostrils. Actually, it's a two-way deal. I have given my art life. But more importantly – my art has given me life…

So far, admittedly, the bread and butter has come from the proceeds of my business sale. But the capital is dwindling and won't last forever. I'm not sure exactly what I'm going to do, but I have some plans. Maybe something on which both the quiet, content fellow *and* the go-getter can collaborate!

Happily Ever After…

I would be lying if I said that my depression was totally over. I'm still medicating and meditating. But something has changed. When it comes, I tackle the depression from a different point of view. My approach was wrong back in Durban. The old either/or approach; either you were happy or you were sad. I have come to realise that there is no absolute depression. Hidden in the depths of depression is also a seed of happiness, a silver lining. If it weren't for depression, after all, I would never have embarked on this Quest. If my life had not once seemed so meaningless, it would not now feel so full of meaning.

POINTS OF VIEW:
UPSIDE DOWN

Maybe in our consumer society depression is undervalued (and happiness overvalued). Maybe the myth of absolute happiness has been too well marketed, the big smiling American dream too thoroughly peddled. It's so easy to believe that just over the hill there is a fairy tale life waiting for us. A life where we will live every moment happily ever after. If only we could get there…

Maybe depression has been the victim of marginalisation and repression like the rest of the Excludeds. To be depressed today is simply not acceptable. If you are depressed you must change yourself immediately. A billion dollar industry is waiting eagerly to help you. Therapists, medication, gurus, books. **10 Fast Steps to Overcome Depression. The How-To Manual of Lasting Happiness. Beating the Blues Once and For All**. All screaming out that it is *not* okay to be depressed.

In recent months I've come to believe that a large part of my depression in Durban was actually caused by being *depressed about being depressed*. It's not cool to be depressed. On the days when I was down, I would feel painfully guilty about it. I would dread the long-lost friend's phonecall, with the obligatory, "How are you, Chris?" In my mind all I heard was, "How *happy* are you, Chris?" Admitting, "Well actually, I'm not really happy at all right now," was just not an acceptable option. Depression has failure written all over it in glaring neon.

I do still get depressed. But I'm finding that if I just accept it, and say, "Well, maybe it's okay to feel like this, right now," the depression is that much more bearable. On more than one occasion it has even disappeared altogether…

The Missing Link

Besides my art, one of the great pleasures in my life at the moment is taking trips to Bhutan. I managed to get one of those Frequent Flyer deals that allows me to go back and forth regularly between Cape Town International airport and Thimphu International. The last trip was particularly interesting…

A winter wind blew from the north as I made my way down Sawadee Avenue. It carried a sting from the snow-clad peaks and I pulled my beanie over my ears. People bustled past, bundled in blankets. It was a Saturday morning and tribal folk from the hills had come into Thimphu to stock up with provisions. The city dwellers' wares spilled out onto the pavements in a kaleidoscope of golds, crimsons and browns.

John was already sipping tea when I got to the teahouse. "Chris! How are you, old chap? Haven't seen you for ages." His smile was genuine. A girl with red hair, reading an English newspaper, looked up as I pulled out a chair.
"Pretty damn cold, huh? I'm told it gets worse."
"Not so bad in my guesthouse. They keep fires burning all night."
I ordered some tea. John looked at me searchingly and then said, "So tell me about that theory you were working on; the one about holism. I'm eager to hear".
"Not much to tell. It didn't really work out."
"Why not? What happened – you were so excited about it?"
I took a sip of tea, resolved that I wasn't in a rush to go anywhere and started explaining. "It all started when I realised that the gap between the Includeds and Excludeds needed to be closed. The objects and subjects. I thought that if I found a big enough whole everything could be included and my problem would be solved".

"Sounds ambitious. So what went wrong?"
"Well, eventually I arrived at what I thought was the *whole* whole, but then I found a hole – without the "w" you understand – inside that. It was just a part of an even greater whole. And that would probably turn out to be part of an even greater whole. The all-inclusive whole is an impossibility."
John's eyes lit up at this and his voice intensified, "Ever heard of Kurt Gödel?"
"Heard the name before… but I can't say in what context."
"He was the greatest mathematician of the last century," John said, clearly on his favourite topic again. "Astounded the whole

world with his Incompleteness Theorem. Basically, he proved that you can never have a complete set of all the rules of mathematics. For, if you get to the point where you say that the set is complete, then it will definitely be inconsistent – harbour internal contradictions. The only way to solve the inconsistency is to bring in another rule that is outside the present set. So it's always either inconsistent or it's incomplete. That's why his theory is called the Incompleteness Theorem. The inconsistency option would have amounted to mathematical suicide!" John paused and looked down into his tea cup.
"So, what he was saying was that you can never have the complete whole?" I asked.
"Yip, that's it. Trying to find the biggest whole that includes all is like trying to find the biggest number. Can't be done!"

It was comforting that a top mathematician had come up against the same problem. John and I spent the rest of the morning catching up on other news. At one point a pretty English girl came in and pulled up a chair at our table. She taught English at the same school as John, and had been in Bhutan for two years. It was a pleasant morning.

At lunchtime I departed. John bid farewell and, as I was leaving, he suddenly said to me in an uncharacteristically calm tone, "Always remember: the infinity that can be defined is not the eternal infinity". I had never looked at it that way but I could see that it made a lot of sense. The very act of defining something made it finite in a way, so its quality of infinity would cease. Simple, but pretty profound at the same time.

As I walked back to the guesthouse the words bounced around my head. *The infinity that can be defined is not the eternal infinity.* It had a vaguely familiar ring to it. Almost like I'd heard it somewhere before. But I didn't know where.

I had a Thai green curry for lunch and afterwards swapped a few simple sentences with the guesthouse owner, whom I had got to know quite well. His English was slowly improving but, given that I had learnt almost nothing of his language, it would still be quite a way before we could have a proper conversation.

The wind had picked up by the evening and icy wisps managed to penetrate the wooden walls of my room. I climbed into bed early and pondered for a while the day's events. It had been good to see John again. He seemed to be very well this time. Not that he hadn't been well on previous trips, but there definitely seemed to have been something different this time. I couldn't quite put my finger on it.

Before blowing out the butter lamp, I reached for my copy of the **Tao te Ching**. The book always accompanied me on my trips to Bhutan. The wisdom in the words still captivated me. I turned to page one and started reading. I was tired and the light was dim. As my eyes met the print, the first sentence jumped up at me.

The Tao that can be told
is not the eternal Tao.

That was it! That's where I'd hear the words before. The infinity that can be defined is not the eternal infinity.

The next morning was grey and windy and I pulled on an extra jersey before venturing out. The streets were quieter than yesterday but it still took me a good ten minutes to cover the few blocks to the Wisdom Shoppe. I always got a warm fuzzy feeling when I first caught sight of the shop tucked away at the end of the road, and today was no exception.

As I got closer I saw the "Do Not Disturb" sign on the door and felt a jolt of disappointment. The door had recently been repainted and, at the top, a set of small brass letters had been hammered into the wood: MEDITATION. I smiled; business must be going well for Ms Samsara D Rampochee!

Just then I heard voices from inside and I peeped through the windows. With the weather so cold, the panes of the windows had fogged up a little. The interior was dimly lit and I couldn't see much at all, but the voices persisted, muffled over the wind. One voice was Sam's, but I couldn't make out the other. Nor could I hear what they were saying.

I was about to step away from the window, conscious that I shouldn't be eavesdropping, when suddenly the wind dropped and the other voice (not Sam's) reached my ears from the interior. An electric jolt went through my being! There was no mistaking that Cambridge accent. It was the voice of John.

As I turned to leave, I glanced one last time at the newly painted door. And that's when it caught my eye. There was one brass letter missing. It must have fallen off at some point. The sign now said: MEDI ATION.

For an instant I thought that maybe the missing letter had not been a T, but rather a C, and that Sam was now dispensing Chinese *medication* rather than *meditation*.

But when I got home that evening I knew what the sign really stood for. It stood neither for medication nor meditation. It stood for exactly what it said – MEDIATION. And when I looked it up in **The Concise Oxford Dictionary** I got:

...to form connecting link between...

And then I knew.

the end
(of the beginning)

MEDICATION MEDITATION
MEDICATION MEDITATION
MEDICATION MEDITATION
MEDICATION MEDITATION
MEDICATION MEDITATION
MEDICATION MEDITATION
MEDIATION
MEDIATION
MEDIATION
MEDIATION
MEDIATION
MEDIATION
MEDIATION
MEDIATION

"mediation – to form connecting link between"
The Concise Oxford Dictionary

CHRISTOPHER

PHILOSOPHER ©

"philosopher – person skilled in philosophy or one of its branches"

The Concise Oxford Dictionary

A MAN OF LETTERS

SOURCES

Abram, David — **The Spell of the Sensuous**
Vintage Books, 1997

Blackstone, Judith — **Zen for Beginners**
Writers and Readers, 1986

Bohm, David — **Wholeness and the Implicate Order**
Routledge, 1996

Bolen, Jean — **The Tao of Psychology**
Harper San Francisco, 1982

Capra, Fritjof — **The Tao of Physics**
Shambhala, 2000
Uncommon Wisdom
Flamingo, 1989

Clément, Catherine — **Theo's Odyssey**
Flamingo, 1999

Deringer, David — **The Alphabet: A Key to the History of Mankind**
Laurier Books, 1997

Descartes, René — **Discourse on Methods and the Meditations**
Penguin, 1968

Durant, Will — **The Story of Philosophy**
Pocket Books, 1961

Gaarder, Jostein — **Sophie's World**
Phoenix, 1995

Gordon, W Terrence — **Saussure for Beginners**
Writers and Readers, 1996

Grigg, Ray — **The Tao of Zen**
Alva Press, 1999

Hawking, Stephen — **A Brief History of Time**
Bantam Books, 1988

Hoff, Benjamin — **The Tao of Pooh Bear**
Mandarin, 1982

Hoffman, Edward — **The Hebrew Alphabet – A Mystical Journey**
Chronicle Books, 1998

Hofstadter, Douglas — **Gödel, Escher, Bach: The Eternal Golden Braid**
Basic Books, 1999

Hope, Jane — **Introducing Buddha**
Icon Books, 1999

Hospers, John — **An Introduction to Philosophical Analysis**
Routledge, 1990

Ifrah, Georges — **The Universal History of Numbers**
John Wiley and Sons, 2000

Jung, Carl — **Synchronicity**
Princeton University Press, 1973

Kaplan, Robert — **The Nothing that Is**
Oxford University Press, 2000

Laing, RD — **The Divided Self**
Viking Press, 1991

Lefton, Lester — **Psychology (Second Edition)**
Allyn and Bacon, 1982

Man, John — **Alpha Beta**
Headline, 2000

Mitchell, Stephen (translator) — **Tao Te Ching**
Kyle Cathie, 2000

Osborne, Richard — **Philosophy for Beginners**
Writers and Readers, 1992
Introducing Eastern Philosophy
Icon Books, 2000

Page, Michael — **Understanding the Power of Ch'I**
Thorsons, 1994

Pirsig, Robert — **Zen and the Art of Motorcycle Maintenance**
Corgi Books, 1987
Lila
Corgi Books, 1992

Russell, Bertrand — **History of Western Philosophy**
Holiday House, 1984

Shlain, Leonard — **The Alphabet versus the Goddess**
Penguin, 1998

Shorto, Russel — **Saints and Madmen**
Henry Holt, 1999

Spencer, Lloyd — **Introducing Hegel**
Icon Books, 1999

Suzuki, DT — **Manual of Zen Buddhism**
Grove Press, 1987

van der Post, Laurens **Jung and the Story of our Time**
Random House, 1976

von Franz, Marie-Louise **Time, Rhythm and Repose**
Thames and Hudson, 1997

Wilhelm, Richard **The Pocket I Ching**
Arkana, 1984

Wilson, Colin **CG Jung: Lord of the Underworld**
Harper Collins, 1988

Zeppa, Jamie **Beyond the Sky and the Earth**
Pan Books, 2000

WEBSITES

http://www.philosophers.co.uk/
http://classics.mit.edu/index.html
http://www.zhongwen.com
http://www.theo.tu-cottbus.de/Wolke/eng/Subjects/subject972.html
http://etext.leeds.ac.uk/leibniz/leibniz.htm#index-div2-N-30330963
http://groups.google.com/groups?hl=en&group=humanities.philosop
hy.objectivism

OTHER

A nine day retreat at the Buddhist Retreat Centre in Ixopo, South Africa, led by Rob Nairn during 2001.